THE PEOPLE
SIDE OF
LEAN THINKING

Also by Robert Brown

THE PEOPLE
SIDE OF
LEAN THINKING

A Practical Guide to Change, Employee Engagement and Continuous Improvement

Robert Brown

bp books

Published by bp books
11700 Mukilteo Speedway #201-1084
Mukilteo WA 98275
USA

Cover design by Gaylord Thompson

Printed in the United States of America

Library of Congress Control Number: 2011910902

ISBN 0-983-67681-X
EAN-13 978-0-9836768-1-2

To my colleagues now and
from times past,
thank you.
And to the memory of my friend
Robert (Robin) Halley VII
who set my career on course.

YOU

Although *The People Side of Lean Thinking* was written for leaders and managers, anyone, no matter what their corporate level who wants to positively impact how well the work gets done and how to ensure an engaged work force, will benefit from reading this book.

The author spent the summer between high school and college working at the historic Ford Motor Company Rouge assembly plant in Dearborn, Michigan making Mustangs. His motivation to succeed in college was greatly enhanced from this experience. At the same time, however, he was productively exposed to the rigors of manual labor, fast production schedules, mandatory overtime, the dance of management and labor, dirt, noise, darkness and grime, and the high cost of mistakes (he once welded a part *to* the assembly line rather than on it).

Since then, he has been a front-line worker, manager and leader, and an independent performance enhancement consultant. What Bob has learned about people, about Lean Thinking, and about leaders and followers will provide you with considerable insight into how people work together to accomplish the seemingly impossible. Learning and using the tools and concepts presented here will help you to become the kind of leader the world needs you to be.

The book is divided into four parts. The first, Prepare the People, is focused on what every business should be doing to enable employees to thrive in a supportive environment.

Second is Respect the People. This section covers the importance of paying attention to the human element as process improvement change initiatives are being put into place.

The next section is Grow the People. Continuous development of employees should be taking place in concert with continuous process improvement. When employees are growing, the business will be growing.

The last portion is More to Do. These are topics that will round out your people side skills for the benefit of your employees and your paying customers.

Each section is further divided into stand-alone topics. You can extrapolate this information to your business and see with your own eyes what can be accomplished. You will also learn how to productively enlist the eyes of others to help everyone find and eliminate waste and create new ways to increase customer value.

FOCUS

Customers believe that the products and services you offer have value. They are willing to drive through the rain, wander up and down aisles, stand in a checkout line and open their wallets. If your customers are patients, they're willing to put even their lives in your hands. Truly understand what your customers value and your business has a good chance of success.

Similarly, employees are willing to endure bumper to bumper commutes, interminable meetings, a gulped-down lunch and at times obnoxious co-workers to pocket that paycheck at the end of the week. Understand what your employees value and your business has an increased chance of success.

The theme of this book is that employees are customers too; that they are just as important for success as paying customers and that treating them as well as paying customers will significantly improve business. This philosophy can be put simply:

The company is loyal to employees.
Employees are loyal to customers.
Customers are loyal to the company.

A sub-theme of this book is a Lean Thinking rule-of-thumb: *Most processes contain at least 50 percent waste*. If we apply this rule to day-to-day management, you can see the issue. This management waste is magnified when implementing any change—but especially with a quality change like Lean Thinking. Ordinarily, we pay people to *do* their jobs, not focus on improving them. We will strive to make every employee a change agent, someone who is on the constant lookout for ways to eliminate waste and to add value.

The general focus of this book is Lean Thinking, although it could have been any change effort. Change adds wide-ranging pressure on all leaders and managers exacerbating everyday errors and omissions. If and when recognized, these missteps can be addressed, but more likely they are missed, and mistakes multiply.

Anyone working with others can use the ideas, tools and concepts covered here. However, the book assumes some familiarity with Lean Thinking and the Toyota Production System. If you don't have working knowledge of this area, Google will be your friend; use it often. You may have to do the same with other topics we will cover by accessing some of the references along the way. Terms with a different font when first used can be found in the glossary.

Lean experts abound who believe that implementing Lean is most effectively begun during a crisis. The idea is that management rushes in when a platform catches on fire, teaches the tools of Lean, applies them and achieves fantastic success; then this new way takes hold. Implementing Lean during a crisis or to avert one is usually a good idea. However, this approach is unnecessary and may cause additional problems such as resistance to the changes, conflicts and good people leaving.

Lean Thinking does not depend on a burning platform, a siege environment, a "for us or against us" mentality or roaming the halls looking for late adopters.

Lean and other change efforts can work without such dramatics if you include employees in the right way. This means enlisting their help to define a grander and more emotionally compelling future and together finding the best ways of getting there.

Motivation is a dual concept; on one hand motivation is moving away from a negative and on the other it is moving toward a positive. Psychosocial research clearly supports that it is more motivating to move toward a positive goal than it is to avoid a negative situation. If that motivation is intrinsic as well as extrinsic, then all the better.

Change guru John Kotter emphasizes creating a sense of urgency to promote change. This is accomplished best when employees understand the problem and focus on the positives of the opportunity rather than the negatives of the problem.

Since human interactions are multi-faceted, a second sub-theme of this book is to make the invisible visible and the complex transparent. We will examine clearly defined, concrete, step-by-step behavioral models and tools to manage employees, including problem solving, directing, team building and discipline.

Becoming a Lean Leader:

Leader - - - - - - - - - -➤ Teacher

Teacher - - - - - - - - - -➤ Student

Student = Learning = Change

You must change to become an effective Lean Leader

An important Lean Thinking concept is visual control. We will apply this to leadership by using lists, formulas and models whenever we can.

Implementing Lean Thinking poorly will result in employees feeling that their work is not currently adequate, that it may never be adequate, and that if this change effort continues, they will eventually lose their jobs.

If you manage the process well, however, implementing Lean Thinking will enable every employee to know that their work has value. Managing well means that employees define their work as adding value for the customer, value for their coworkers and value for themselves. An added benefit is that they will enjoy their jobs, identify waste and continually improve how the work gets done.

However, many people dislike the term "waste" for non-value-added activity. Even the term "non-value-added" is irritating and frustrating when applied to the work someone has been doing for years. Although for the most part in this book I have retained the classic terms to ensure clarity, together we could begin the convention of using "L activities" for any behavior that has been designed to add value for paying customers and employees and "NL (for non-lean) activities" that would fit the current definition of non-value added, waste or any action that hasn't focused on customer value. Word usage can be critical. It's all about people.

Our goal is that you become a better leader and manager by constantly eliminating your NL activities and helping employees add value with theirs.

Finally, the ultimate goal of the people side of Lean Thinking is fulfilling human potential, congruent with the goal of perfection for continuous improvement. What would fulfilling human potential look like? How would you do it? Do you think how you lead today could get close to fulfilling the human potential of your employees? Make some of the changes suggested in this book; you may be pleasantly surprised.

Seek perfection in your processes, in your employees and in your leadership no matter what your level.

LEAN THINKING AND PEOPLE

I began writing this book in my head about five years ago after observing a critical incident. We were conducting a week-long Rapid Process Improvement Workshop (RPIW) at an outpatient medical clinic. My job as the workshop leader was to make sure we would reach our goal, which was creating standard work for medical assistants.

We accomplished a lot over the first three days and were testing how well the medical assistants followed the newly created standard work.

With clipboard and stopwatch in hand I was following an assistant and checking off each completed step of the process. She was within a second or two of perfection. Suddenly she took an unscheduled detour, adding at least twenty steps and more than ninety seconds to the cycle time; totally ignoring our well-defined protocol. I soundly criticized her for not following standard work and ruining our data. She smiled.

What happened was halfway to the lab, the assistant noticed an elderly woman in a wheelchair anxiously patting the pockets of her coat. She quickly walked over, knelt at the woman's side and asked if she needed help. The patient said she couldn't find the information sheet she had brought to show her doctor. Together, they found the correct coat pocket, retrieved the information and all was well.

The assistant added significant value just by this one simple act.

However, standard work had not been followed. Her aberrant behavior had increased cycle time and upset the schedule for every downstream activity of that value stream. What was she to do? She was following her heart not standard work.

Lean Thinking

Time is the critical measure of Lean Thinking. We must standardize the time for tasks and reduce the lead-time to deliver a requested product or service.

Researchers at MIT coined the term "Lean" to capture Toyota's efforts to reduce waste.

A people-focused marketing company might have created a more engaging expression like "workers' wisdom."

Taiichi Ohno's idea, and that of Henry Ford before him, was simple: Reduce the timeline for product delivery by removing any wastes in production. Waste is defined as anything that does not add value for the customer.

Identifying waste is the first task and eliminating waste is second—to be followed by endlessly continuing this improvement effort.

According to Ohno, there are seven types of waste:
- Overproduction
- Waiting
- Transporting
- Over processing
- Inventories
- Moving
- Defects

His method to eliminate these wastes was simple and in two parts:
1. Just-in-time
2. Autonomation

"Just-in-time" is exactly that. Nothing is done until the moment it needs to be done. "Autonomation" is automation with a human touch. In its basic form, it is a machine that will automatically stop if an error is made.

The conceptual roots of the Toyota Production System (TPS) go back to Sakichi Toyoda's loom in the early 20th century, which was designed to automatically stop if a thread broke.

Beginning during the post World War Two years, Toyota experimented with many tools to continue the effort to eliminate waste. These included:

- Baka-Yoke (fool-proofing) now known as Poka-Yoke (mistake-proofing)
- Asking "why" five times
- Kanban (information)
- Andon (visual control)
- Level Loading (the work)
- Standard Work

Many of today's organizations learn Lean tools, measure process data, benchmark from the best of the best and otherwise do everything possible to eliminate unstable processes. Standardizing the work is the mantra.

That medical assistant was told to follow standard work but didn't. She ignored what she was supposed to do, yet she clearly made the right decision. It was obvious we were missing something important in our definition of standard work.

A few anticipated this issue. Bob Emiliani has written extensively about lean behavioral issues and he, my colleague Rudy Williams, and other lean experts have proposed that ineffective behavior should be defined as an eighth waste.* Behavioral waste is any behavior that inhibits value-added work. Behavioral waste (or NL activity) includes and can result in inadequate training, mistakes, confusion, poor teamwork, low morale, diminished job satisfaction, fear, ineffective rewards and, unfortunately, many more emotions, behaviors and

---

* A more detailed look at Lean and people interactions can be found in Brown's *Lean Thinking 4.0*.

outcomes that make employees miserable. Critical for our purposes is to understand that this eighth waste idea includes leadership and management behavior as well as employee and work team behaviors.

We now come face to face with the profound but neglected realities of the people side of Lean Thinking.

People

Having people perform the work rather than machines is problematic. What must be different to be successful with flesh and blood workers compared to the metal and oil variety?

When people become employees they walk through the door with a complex set of needs and expectations. We must be able to meet those needs and expectations and motivate employees to do their jobs well and, at the same time, improve how the work gets done.

Leaders will be challenged by the people side of Lean Thinking. They have to learn how to add value from the viewpoint of both the paying customer and the employee customer. Leaders also have to identify and eliminate their personal leadership waste and the collective management team waste.

Our guiding leadership principle is doing whatever it takes to enhance value for customers *and* employees.

Leaders don't have to do it all. We're in this together. There is no right way, no standard way, no best thinking handed down from corporate to be applied everywhere.

Along with their needs and expectations, employees bring an untapped store of wisdom and creativity ready to be shared; if asked.

How to Use This Book

I learned a lot from formal and informal talks with Chihiro Nakao, (protégé of Taiichi Ohno, former group manager of Toyota, and current Chair of Shingijutsu Consulting). At one of our management report-outs of kaizen results, he pointed to the dozens of sheets of data thumb tacked to the wall and with a grand sweep of his arm, declared them to be lies. He was clearly saying that everything written was a lie.

This means value streams, flow diagrams and data listed on a. The reason is that reports, charts, diagrams visibility wall and similar documents are in varying degrees abstractions, summaries, averages, estimates, and, at the least, not what is happening in the work place *at this moment*.

Sensei Nakao was always insisting we see with our own eyes (genchi genbutsu). Seeing and actually doing were the only ways to truly understand.

That idea applies to this book. Don't automatically trust anything I say. Go out and see processes and activities for yourself, make notes in the book margins as you go along, create your own guide and test your knowledge every day by continued seeing and doing.

I also will say "should" a lot. Take this to mean you should think about my point and do what you think is best, test what you do and keep improving it.

Of course, when I say don't trust anything I say, that doesn't mean ignore it. I'm relating what I saw; much of it I believe, you will see too.

Most leaders truly believe that they are part of a learning organization. Many endorse comprehensive 360-degree evaluations complete with 30-page summaries of strengths, weaknesses, blind spots and the like expressed in charts, lists, graphs and other data measured to the third decimal point. (Imagine what Sensei Nakao would have to say about that!) Few leaders ask employees what they as leaders should be improving; fewer still would get honest answers. This barrier to effectively working together should be unacceptable to every competent leader.

It will take many eyes to see the waste that *your* leader/manager actions create.

In fact, I once asked Sensei Nakao how to identify leadership waste and I must confess I didn't understand his answer. My guess is that even he hadn't given much thought to the unstable nature of leadership behavior.

> The essence of TPS is that each individual employee is given the opportunity to find problems *in his own way of working*, to solve them and to make improvements.
> Yoshihito Wakamatsu and Tessuo Kondo
> Students of Taiichi Ohno

This book will give you ideas and proven tools to use. A few are only briefly introduced, enough so you can decide if you want to go to the source to learn more. I hope the book also inspires you to create your own tools.

A couple of years ago, I designed a tool to create vision statements. A colleague asked if I would help her create a vision for her team. My suggestion was for her team members to use the tool together, so the vision was by everyone for everyone. I believe this has always been the actual process of the Toyota Production System. Employees developed one tool at a time over the years as knowledge grew and needs were identified. TPS and employees grew step by step together.

Most organizations take the most recent ideas and tools of TPS and teach them in bulk to employees, often in classrooms, neglecting the huge benefit of individuals and teams learning and discovering problems and solutions with one another as needs are uncovered.

Another TPS mantra, "just-in-time," should be applied when learning Lean. This book will help you to know what to do, and when, on the people side.

The book design also includes maximum white space for you to note your thoughts, what you plan to do, what you did, the results and what you will do next time.

Take notes too. Make this a living document of your emphasis on the people side of Lean Thinking.

Our target is for you to be able to:
1. Inspire your employees to become change agents
2. Enable them to become change agents
3. Ensure that they will always be change agents
4. Effectively reduce management, team and employee waste

More specifically, the desired outcomes are:
- High levels of measured productivity
- "Mistake-proofed" leadership
- High-performing teams
- High levels of staff satisfaction
- Daily process improvements
- Loyal customers, both employees and those paying the overhead

What you will see with your own eyes are such desirable activities as:
1. Specific steps taken to create teams when needed
2. Parallel thinking used to solve problems
3. Work unit vision statements and personal mission statements
4. Team agreements and peers holding each other accountable
5. Formal and informal continuous improvement efforts
6. Team members giving feedback to one another

The workplace will practically run itself.

PREPARE THE
PEOPLE

Our assumption is that you want to begin using Lean Thinking to improve your company's efficiency or that you already have. This first section will enable you to prepare employees for Lean type improvements or, if you're not making these changes, to help them enjoy their work more while they improve the value of their work.

Our initial focus is guided by the ideas in *Toyota Talent* by Jeffrey Liker and David Meier. They emphasize that Toyota expects to mold the individual to fit the needs of the company and at the same time to support the interests of the employee.

They further explain that the Toyota Production System identifies process problems while Toyota's Human System engages people who are willing and able to solve process problems.

Critical to this joint effort are managers who consider teaching to be a primary function of their jobs.

Liker and Meier also report:

> *We are constantly frustrated by companies that see Lean as a tool kit and do not understand that the main value of Lean projects is in developing people who can solve problems and make daily improvements.*

Our goal is to enable you to prepare a working environment that performs as well as or better than any in the world today.

THE ORGANIZATION

This first section looks at the critical components of an organization that is ready to make big changes. It will describe the makeup of a Lean-ready company without the need of burning platforms.

Toyota has an enviable history of engaging employees in continuous improvement. They emphasize horizontal relationships between employees, grouping them by specialties even across functional and geographic boundaries. Toyota also promotes a strict vertical hierarchy, but encourage employees to push back. (This contradiction is explained in a *Harvard Business Review* article, The Contradictions That Drive Toyota's Success, June 2008.)

Toyota sets seemingly impossible goals yet ensures that employees feel that each of them will contribute to achieving those goals. Employees believe that "Toyota will make tomorrow a better day" and view obstacles only as challenges that will be overcome.

Teamwork is stressed. Appropriate alternative work is found for lagging employees; they are not automatically dismissed. On-the-job training is preferred. Managers are evaluated more on process performance and learning than on results. Personal relationships are critical as is the dissemination of information to all parts of the organization.

Some companies implementing Lean seem to have overlooked these people elements. They add Lean Thinking as another layer to what they do currently or use Lean Thinking as their new management system, but without the respecting the people half of the method. It is my belief that the majority of failed or weak implementations of Lean Thinking is because of inadequate employee preparation.

Additionally, I believe that the inability to sustain Lean is due to leadership not supporting, emphasizing or rewarding the less visible incremental gains achieved by individuals and work teams.

Management must do more than teach Lean tools and encourage workers to use them; management must change itself in order to prepare, respect and develop their employees.

The *Harvard Business Review* article warned that organizations that wish to follow Toyota's success have a difficult task:
- They must embrace contradictions as a way of life.
- They must develop "routines" to cope with contradictions.

- And management must encourage criticism and be open to it.

Ready to improve the people side?

The Company Vision
and Mission

Sam Walton had a vision, as did other notables including Hannibal, Joan of Arc and Thomas Jefferson. A vision is a promise of a better tomorrow if...

There are a lot of ifs...
>   If we believe in the vision
>   If the vision is inspiring
>   If we are willing to work toward the vision
>   If the vision is understandable
>   If the vision is realistic
>   If the company is moving toward the vision
>   If we even know what the vision is

A good vision can get you going, keep you moving when your face is in the mud and most importantly, solidify the teamwork needed to get the job done.

Your company vision sets the stage for what people think and do. All decisions should reflect that vision. Visions should be short, vivid and inspiring. Usually they are long, vapid and boring and contain everything but the kitchen sink, the opposite of inspiring.

Some of my favorite visions from years past are:
>   Ford: Democratize the automobile
>   Nike: Crush Adidas
>   Honda: We will destroy Yamaha
>   Stanford: Become the Harvard of the
>   West

It's easy to see what these organizations wanted to accomplish.

A company vision is often the product of the administration department or the board, with minimal input from other stakeholders, such as employees or customers. Sometimes it's purchased from a media consultant. Usually a vision describes a future where the company is the industry leader contributing to the welfare of the community with admirable diversity and good will to all.

This is an effective vision: *Our products will transform how the world learns*. Of course, if your company makes small fasteners for the aerospace industry, how inspiring can making a three-quarter inch bolt be? Maybe a vision like this would work: *We will soar into space and bring everyone home safely*.

The mission statement is where you explain the details, like this: We provide the best shopping experience by never allowing the customer to leave dissatisfied, by providing the largest range of choices, by having the most diverse, best trained staff, by having the lowest prices, by giving everyone chocolate, etc., etc.

Your mission statement should further clarify your vision and outline the ways in which you intend to get there. Since you're reading this book, eliminating waste and engaging employees should be part of your mission statement.

Your company may not have a compelling vision. If that is the case, don't worry. Having no vision or a poor one is rarely a handicap for two reasons. One, your competition probably doesn't have a vision statement. If they do have a vision statement, it is probably a poor one. Two, most employees of large companies have no idea what the vision is anyway.

If you want to make your company the best it can be, create a *great* vision statement. If you have one that needs improvement, improve it.

If you run a small company or a department within a large organization, you absolutely need a vision statement. In the later section on workgroups, you can review how to create one.

A good vision statement can make a significant difference for decision-making and employee engagement. My wife works for a medical company without a vision statement (as far as we can tell). She created a personal vision/mission to help direct her job: *Do whatever is in the patient's best interest.* This enables her to do the right thing when situations become complicated. Your employees need something similar.

○

Leadership

I was drafted during the Vietnam War. I never saw combat, but did observe how authoritarian, top-down systems worked. Being near the bottom, no one asked what I thought or even cared what I thought. If I tried to explain what I was thinking, I was quickly told that I wasn't paid to think.

We were supposed to follow regulations, but few of us did to any great degree. Our operating principle was we could do pretty much anything we wanted unless something went wrong. When that happened, we were in trouble if we hadn't followed the regs. Blame was always finger pointing at the other guy or, if the breach was serious enough, to the next higher level.

This follow-the-rules-or-you're-in-trouble system works reasonably well during a crisis and if you have enough manpower to overcome the built-in inefficiencies of poor communication and from-the-top and from-a-distance decision-making.

Unless you're the general of an old-fashioned army though, you're better off creating a system where decisions are made at the lowest level possible, with constant feedback up and down and from side to side as events unfold. (I understand that even in the military these days, decisions are made at lower levels.)

Leaders should be busy creating an effective decision-making system and not making so many decisions of their own.

> The root of the Toyota Way is to be dissatisfied with the status quo; you have to ask constantly, *"Why are we doing this?"*
>
>   Katsuaki Watanabe
>
> Which should include why leaders do what they are doing.

Information exchange should be constant. The generic conversation to figure things out begins with, "This is what I think" and continues with, "What do *you* think?" Bosses should listen more than they speak.

In the most effective businesses, the word "we" is heard a lot. Leaders must be the ones to ensure this happens.

○

Fat Behaviors

If leaders are to successfully implement Lean, they must begin with themselves. Professor Bob Emiliani, Central Connecticut State University, has a lot of thoughts about Lean leadership. We will look at only one of his many leadership ideas, fat and lean behaviors.

Fat behaviors are those that create waste and lean are those behaviors which have been proven effective.

For example, yelling at an employee is fat behavior. Yelling may get the job done, but it creates waste by fostering thoughts and feelings that are probably not in the best interest of the company.

Another fat behavior is delegating work in an unclear manner. Poor delegating can lead to employees making mistakes and the job not getting done correctly and on time.

Other fat behaviors include not being available when needed, not rewarding performance when appropriate, belittling, not listening, talking too much, leading boring and ineffective meetings and being late.

Lean behaviors, on the other hand, are those that promote employees to be the best they can be. Examples are active listening, coaching after mistakes, relating to employees as people and clearly defining goals and leader accountability.

Our rule-of-thumb is that any *un-leaned* process, including leadership and management processes, begins with at least 50 percent waste. Before you ask employees to Lean their activities, take a look at your own.

Start a list of your leadership behaviors. How well do you delegate? How efficient are your meetings? Do you talk too much? How much information do you need before you make a decision? Do you thank people enough? In the right way?

Ask colleagues about your leadership behaviors. Then ask subordinates. Make a list of your fat behaviors, identify the most mission-critical one or two, define your desired Lean behaviors, make them public and start working on improving yourself. And make sure every other leader does the same.

○

Fail Forward Fast

Two points you may not have thought about:
1. You should hire people who are willing to fail.
2. You should create a culture where failure is acceptable, even endorsed.

Why would I do that, you may be thinking.

In Lean, speed is critical. Speed to:
- Get the product into the customer's hands.
- Fix a problem.
- Find better ways of getting the job done.

If you want your people to learn quickly, you must encourage them to try, perhaps fail, try again and maybe fail again, and try some more. Failure should be a *good* outcome (or at least, not an awful one).

Perfection isn't found in the design; it is uncovered in the learning.

Ray Dalio, who founded the largest hedge fund in the world, has a set of principles by which the fund operates. Part of one principle is this formula:

Pain + Reflection = Progress

He wants his people willing and able to admit and reflect on mistakes, to the (perhaps excessive) point of running assessment sessions where employees discuss their mistakes.

Were any of your employees hired for their pain tolerance? How about their interest in and ability to reflect on their mistakes and their willingness to make changes? How many of your employees are truly interested in progress?

Human behavior is never going to operate at a Six Sigma level of error, yet most organizations do not handle errors in productive ways. You should manage so employees are encouraged to admit mistakes, fix them, learn from them and move on.

The worst way of making this happen is to tell people that this is what you want. People are not designed to comfortably accept failure and its dire anticipated consequences.

Remember sitting in school waiting with the other kids for the teacher to hand out grades on a recent assignment? No matter how prepared you were, anxiety about the results roiled in your stomach like mini tornados. Receiving lower than the anticipated grade felt lousy, just like making a mistake on the job. That feeling has been ingrained in us from a very early age.

Instead of saying that making mistakes is okay or having meetings to talk about the idea of mistakes or mandatory training to sell the idea that mistakes are acceptable, tell stories about some of the whoppers.

Fred's boss told this story at a staff meeting just before presenting him with the "Fail Forward Fast" award for the week, shaking his hand and giving him the free lunch voucher that came with the award.

Fred tried an experiment last week. He was going to speed up customer service by having customers take a number as they entered the store. At check-out they put themselves in line by the order of their numbers. What a mess. People kept coming to check-out with lower numbers than the people that were already there. Luckily, he only gave out about twenty numbers and told all of them it was just an experiment. Giving them a gift for participating cooled a few hot collars.

Such stories expand the benefits of failing. Learn from failure. Bond better as a team after failures. Become energized after failure.

When Thomas Edison failed in yet another attempt to invent the electric light bulb, he chalked it up as discovering one more way not to do it. If Mr. Genius Thomas Edison can fail . . . seems like that might be okay for others too.

Have failure stories a part of meetings. Tell of some mistakes you've made. Find examples from outside your company and tell those as well.

People respond to stories on an emotional level, which is where failure lives. Pronouncements about accepting failure are a bit of a failure themselves. They don't work. However, the supportive aftermath of failure and a few good stories will.

Learn by trying. Learn by reflecting. Learn by sharing.

○

Heroic Environment

I've never met Rob Lebow. I'd like to. This is his idea:

> *Imagine a place where everyone puts the interests*
> *of others before their own. Where everyone tells*
> *the truth and where trust and mentoring abound.*
> *That place is called an Heroic Environment®.*

I believe this is the kind of place you should work in, a place ready for Lean Thinking or any other major change. The reason?

Trust.

Without trust, organizational change most likely will fail, simple as that.

Lebow has published some helpful books: *A Journey into the Heroic Environment, Lasting Change,* with coauthor William Simon, and an equally good book, *Accountability — Freedom and Responsibility Without Control,* coauthored with Randy Spitzer. These books cover some of the important territory you should know about.

They will help you create an environment in which employees can act without fear. In my military days, we never told our superiors what we were up to. Fear was rampant, as was disinterest and dishonesty.

If bosses act like parents, employees will act like children. Some bosses may defend this approach because employees can act like children. If that's the case, you hired the wrong people or they're just fulfilling your expectations. People tend to act the way you treat them.   Treat your employees right, as accountable adults.

Imagine a company run according to what Lebow calls shared values:

- Treat others with uncompromising truth.
- Lavish trust on your associates.
- Mentor unselfishly.
- Be receptive to new ideas, regardless of their origin.
- Take personal risks for the organization's sake.
- Give credit where it is due.
- Do not touch dishonest dollars.
- Put the interests of others before your own.

Here is his concept:

> *Workers want to feel that they are trusted and appreciated, that they contribute to their organization's success in productive and recognizable ways. They want a workplace where truth, honesty and respect are involved in all business conducted within and by their organizations. If members of an organization are given the opportunity to work in such a place, they will act "Heroically" as a natural course of events.*

To successfully implement Lean Thinking, or any significant change, you should do all you can to create such an environment.

○

Just Culture

Imagine working sixteen-hour days for two weeks to create a national presentation. You finish organizing the slides only minutes before ascending the platform. With a tight stomach and dry mouth, you begin your speech. After an exhausting but exciting thirty minutes, you conclude, hustle off the stage and sink into a seat next to your boss. After a moment, you look over optimistically. She leans toward you and hisses,

> *Slides twelve and thirteen had outdated information that makes us look ridiculous. What's wrong with you? See me in my office first thing Monday. You might want to work on your resume.*

Should grownups be punished for making an honest mistake? Are some mistakes more acceptable than others—why? Do we, should we, expect perfection? How many mistakes are too many? How can we create a safe environment for failing forward fast? When personnel problems arise, is there a best way of handling them that promotes both employees and best outcomes?

The Just Culture algorithm seems ready-made for an organization that seeks to implement Lean Thinking. You want your organization to be comfortable with people trying new ways of working. To do that, you must have a process in place that engenders trust, fairness and a wise (+ practical) understanding of mistakes.

David Marx's Just Culture concept is a good way for you to better understand human nature and how best to deal with our ever-present foibles and follies.

Lean Thinking is an attempt to eliminate error and to respond quickly and appropriately when processing mistakes are made. Similarly, Just Culture provides a way of understanding and responding to people's mistakes.

> Often human error is based on faulty thinking or mis-communication. The more human interactions can be defined and structured with step-by-step or checklist type tools, the more these human elements can be mistake-proofed.
>
> Also see sections on Crucial Conversations and Harnessing the Speed of Thought®

A truism in Lean Thinking is that when a person makes a mistake, it is usually because of an unstable process. That is, people don't want to make a mistake, but the system allowed human limitations to take over (Murphy's Law is alive and flourishing).

People may make errors because they were not well trained for the job. However, they may also make errors because they recklessly ignored that training.

A wise organization, a Just Culture, understands human behavior and takes the appropriate factors into account in responding to mistakes.

The Just Culture algorithm asks three basic questions:
- Did the employee put the company's interest in harm's way?
- Was there a breach of an established rule?
- Did the employee fail to produce an outcome?

From these, the manager can take a set of clearly defined steps to understand and resolve the issue. These steps are followed to determine if the employee simply made an error, took a calculated risk or was behaving recklessly. Depending on what happened, the response can range from consoling to coaching to punishing the employee. The response is thoughtful and transparent, and it should be consistent throughout the organization as standardized management behavior.

Does your company have a productive approach to human error? What tools are used? Is using the tool standard practice for all situations and levels? Have managers been adequately trained to use the tool? Would employees praise how problems are handled?

Create a Just Culture before you move on to other improvement efforts. It is "walking the talk" that you truly value your employees. Compare the relative benefit of putting on an elaborate annual Employee Appreciation Day with creating a system-wide Just Culture. It's a no brainer. Which are you doing?

o

Crucial Conversations

Another basic task for leaders seeking to fulfill employees' potential is to address interpersonal conflicts with a tool of proven value.

Central to that concept is creating a safe way of resolving volatile issues. When tension is high, we tend to go into protect or attack mode, neither of which helps us move to a resolution.

For effective conflict resolution it is necessary to make it safe to talk about any issue.

If you're going to go looking for waste with the goal of successfully eliminating it, you've got to be able to talk about every kind of waste. Chances are, right now, you cannot.

Marriage counselors know that if you can get the two combatants talking in a safe place and in a structured way, even the most estranged couples can overcome their problems and learn to enjoy each other's company again.

The difficulty is the opposing parties do not want to become vulnerable to one another. The more you can provide a safe structure, the easier it is for both parties to take a chance.

The way Crucial Conversations creates a safe structure is for the two parties to dialogue, that is, to create a free flow of information and the exchange of personal perspective all the while moving toward the goal of shared meaning, which then leads to a resolution. What happens is that opposing views, and personal wants and fears, are communicated in order to clarify the issues. If this exchange begins to heat up, participants can note the need to enhance safety and then follow prescribed steps to reestablish safety before continuing. This tool provides concrete ways of evaluating how the dialogue is progressing and how to make it safe.

You may not want group hugs clogging your hallways, but having a safe, structured way of solving problems is a strong asset if you want to do Lean.

The book *Crucial Conversations* is by Kerry Patterson, Joseph Grenny, Ron McMillan and Al Switzler.

Another important concept and resource for overcoming the difficulties of change is the idea of influencing. Read *Influencer* by the same group as *Crucial Conversations* with the addition of another author, David Maxfield.

Before you begin a change effort, make sure you understand the dynamics of change and what is important to people. By doing so, you can greatly enhance the chances that the changes will occur and be sustained. *Influencer* presents high-leverage behaviors and strategies and six sources of influence that combine into a matrix anyone can use to implement change.

The emphasis is on identifying the critical behaviors that will make a difference. They suggest spending as much time as it takes and researching what has worked in similar situations to clarify your targets. Begin by recalling what worked before and as with Lean, run a series of small experiments to confirm your ideas.

The six sources of influence are:
1. Personal motivation—what the individual is prone to do
2. Personal ability—options, strengths and weaknesses
3. Social motivation—what the group tends to do
4. Social ability—helping each other
5. Structural motivation—behavioral options
6. Structural ability—available resources

If you don't know this area or don't use these ideas, you have some homework to do. Learn the story of the Guinea worm, tell it often and use its lessons to grow your organization. Learn how to make improvement inevitable.

○

Creativity and Innovation

Failure is alive and well when we explore new ways of doing things, like implementing Lean Thinking. Innovation experts say that for every 100 creative ideas, only one or two will eventually bear fruit.

If you want to work on failing forward fast, fostering creativity and innovation at your organization is a great way to do it, especially if you share stories about seemingly stupid ideas that succeeded magnificently; bottled water and four-dollar cups of coffee immediately come to mind.

First on our creativity agenda is reviewing Edward de Bono's idea of "mental valleys." We tend to get stuck thinking about things in the same old ways, like a valley where water flows along the bottom and stays there.

Understanding this concept will help you when it's time to talk with employees about waste and value-added work.

Creative people seem to have new ideas simply pop into their heads. Perhaps uncontrollably, they see things differently than other folks much of the time. With the right structure, everyone, to some degree anyway, can become similarly creative.

The way most of us can become more creative is simply to think the same way we always do, but then add one or two more ideas guided by innovation techniques.

Innovation guru Paul Plsek suggests a three-step process:
1. Attention—an intense focus on the object, idea or behavior
2. Escape—move from common to novel
3. Movement—let your mind go everywhere

For example, let's take a look at Sally, who wants to improve interactions at the cash register. She will first pay attention to what currently happens. Sally will not evaluate or judge, just observe. Once she understands what the process is, she will escape, wondering about doing the process differently. She might add one more idea, wondering how this transaction would be done if both customer and cashier were deaf. After doing this with a few different scenarios, she'd allow her mind to move, exploring whatever enters her head.

De Bono calls this lateral thinking, to move out of our mental valleys. Lateral thinking is putting ideas together that don't normally go together, like a plastic bag and the zipper on a suitcase which combine to create a new object, the zip lock bag. With a little guidance, everyone can do this.

Endorsing creativity and innovation can be a two-step process. Step one is to have creativity-innovation sessions to learn the tools, to try them out, to encourage one another and to create stories of great ideas and profound failures.

Once this is accomplished, step two is to create a culture of innovation to support your Lean efforts. Plsek provides us with a way to understand what this means.

He suggests seven key dimensions that should be in place and supported in order to have an effective innovation culture.

They are:

- *Risk taking*—people must feel comfortable taking a risk
- *Resources for innovation*—if people want to do it, they're helped to do it
- *Widely shared knowledge*—tell stories, work in groups, share ideas
- *Specific targets*—work on what is important
- *Tools and techniques*—everyone should learn the tools and use them regularly
- *Reward systems*—meaningfully reward effort and results
- *Rapidly formed relationships*—create and dissolve teams as needed

- Colleague Rudy Williams added an eighth— *Leadership*—create the right kind of energy and direction

Some people are automatically going to see things differently. You must determine how to encourage and support this. Too often, bosses have a mental valley of believing that new ideas only complicate things.

Other people say they're not creative. Maybe not naturally, but with the right structure, they can contribute grand new ways of getting the work done.

Make this wonderful resource grow.

Like many of the ideas we will explore, innovation is one that many companies tend to make into a system-wide initiative. They hire big names, hold big meetings and run big experiential learning seminars.

It is far better to have less renowned training and trainers so employees can learn-by-doing in their work teams. A small acorn can grow a pretty big tree. If you sow a lot of acorns you might get a lot of trees, some of them huge. Don't start with trying to plant a fully-grown tree.

Most people do not see themselves as very creative. Often people think their ideas are nothing special and even when they do; many don't feel comfortable speaking up. Start small, with relaxed expectations so everyone can participate.

Once you have even a moderate culture of innovation, making changes is more like throwing out a few seeds than transplanting a two hundred-ton redwood.

o

Change

Organization development experts report that change initiatives succeed only about a third of the time (and Lean implementation even less than that). By now you should know why: The people were not prepared.

I hope you also are thinking: *People weren't prepared because the organization didn't create a safe, encouraging environment.* Good, let's keep going.

As we noted earlier, change will occur if the current situation is unacceptable and/or if a new outcome is highly attractive. After creating a supportive work culture, the next task in creating the right psychological environment is to have employees sense that the current situation is not acceptable and a new situation will be better.

> Be guided by two critical factors for successful change. One is a well defined and emotionally engaging goal. The other is the meaningful involvement of those who will make the needed changes.

John Kotter wasn't the first with this concept, but he explains it well. The idea is that the need for change may be an intelligent assessment of the situation, but actually changing is an emotional experience. His book, *The Heart of Change* is a classic.

William Bridges in *Transitions*: *Making Sense of Life's Changes* says that the emotional side of change is the "transition" from the known to the unknown, then to the new known. He postulates three stages: Endings, the Neutral Zone (which can be chaotic) and New Beginnings.

A few of the concerns to note are:
Endings
- Am I acknowledging losses?
- Am I communicating enough?
- Do the employees have sufficient and accurate information?
- Are we measuring progress and defining the end (of the old)?

Neutral zone
- Are we accepting the reality of the neutral zone?
- Are we measuring progress?
- Are we safe from more attacks?
- Do people feel supported?

New beginnings
- How are people really feeling?
- Are the new elements clear?
- Are we celebrating?
- Have we re-formed into our new teams?

Ignore the emotional elements of change at your peril. In fact, if you ignore the emotional elements or don't know how to manage them, as my math professor used to say, "You may as well turn in your slide rule and check out a chorus robe." (A slide rule was an ancient mathematical computation device similar in appearance to a short, thick ruler, often worn in holsters by engineering students. They were replaced by handheld calculators, which, I believe, were also worn in holsters by engineering students.)

Kotter notes eight steps to effective change at the organization level:
1. Increase urgency
2. Build the guiding team
3. Get the vision right
4. Communicate for buy-in
5. Empower action
6. Create short-term wins
7. Don't let up
8. Make change stick

In a nutshell, Kotter says, "We see, we feel, we change."

That's our target: To create an organization that supports people's emotional needs, to help them perceive what is critical, to encourage them to try new things to solve important problems, and to work hard *together* to eliminate process waste and improve value.

○

Job vs. Contribution

It is easy for an organization to make the critical error of underestimating how much employees own their jobs.

The common vocational dynamic is managers want employees to take ownership of their jobs. This means workers are accountable for what they do. Then, we implement something like Lean and tell employees that their jobs are not value added and changes need to be made. We do this after insisting the whole time that they take ownership of their jobs.

Bad idea.

If you further promote the idea that it isn't the specific job that is important, but rather meeting the needs of the organization is, you are covertly or maybe not so covertly suggesting that employees are just cogs in the great wheel of production. You don't want to do that either.

If you want to implement Lean or any change, stay away from the idea of job satisfaction or owning the job. Instead, put emphasis on employee contribution.

When you hire people, talk to them about the importance of the organization's vision and mission. Declare how new employees are critical in fulfilling that vision and mission.

Let them know that they were hired to contribute to the mission and that in addition to their work, you need them to bring new ideas that will change how the work is accomplished. And tell them that as the company grows and as *they* grow, their work will evolve, and their contributions will become more and more important.

If you can't truthfully tell them that, and make sure it happens, you have no business hiring them.

We need to know how employees define their roles. Is it simply performing the job as instructed or contributing whatever it takes to fulfill the vision? Employees do not simply do their jobs. They respond emotionally, good and bad, to the work and the work environment. If you want employees to give their all, give them your all; which means creating the kind of work environment that will enable them to fulfill their potential.

Even the lowliest employee has the full complement of human emotions. Respect each of them.

And make sure their boss asks often, maybe every day, "How did it go today?" and, "What can we do to make it better?"

○

Prepare the People
Organization Checklist

The more check-marked boxes the better.

The company has an emotionally engaging
vision statement. ☐

Employees know what the company vision
statement is. ☐

The company has a compelling mission
statement. ☐

Employees use the vision and mission
statements to guide their work. ☐

Employees have influence over how their
work is performed. ☐

Most improvement suggestions come from the
workers rather than from leadership. ☐

Leaders are eliminating their fat behaviors and
acquiring lean behaviors. ☐

Employees give leaders feedback on the
leaders' improvement efforts. ☐

There is a spirit of learning on all levels of the
organization. ☐

The work environment is kind. ☐

Errors are addressed with a standardized and "Just" response. ☐

Difficult conversations achieve satisfying outcomes. ☐

Trying and failing is an accepted way of learning. ☐

Every employee is taught how to be creative. ☐

Every employee is given the support necessary to try innovations on-the-job or in simulations. ☐

Effort, not just results, is rewarded. ☐

Employees define change as part of the job, not a new initiative of some sort. ☐

People see change as something they are in charge of, not something done to them. ☐

Change helps fulfill the vision, not solve a crisis. ☐

People love their jobs because they feel a sense of contribution. ☐

People feel like they're contributing because they know they are an important part of a team doing important work. ☐

Leaders are learning standardized leadership/management tools and models. ☐

THE WORKGROUP

In *Toyota Production System*, Taiichi Ohno often talked about meeting employees' needs. He said, "Do not make isolated islands." And added, "If a worker is alone, there can be no teamwork. Even if there is only enough work for one person, five or six workers should be grouped together to work as a team."

I think that was a brilliant idea. The sense of belonging is a deeply rooted human trait. If the workgroup can provide an important portion of an employee's psychosocial needs, that employee will be better able to meet the needs of the company.

If we stretch our memories back to introductory psychology and sociology classes, we will recall that man is a social animal. Managers need to know what that means in the workplace and make it happen like Ohno would. Does a line worker really work for the customer's benefit or are there other considerations to take into account?

People are not going to sweat blood to reduce process time by eleven seconds for a distant and invisible customer. They will for a teammate.

Over the next few pages, we will explore the most critical area for effectively supporting change, the workgroup.

Teams

Let's begin by conceding what a workgroup really should be—a team. Teams achieve better results. Later, we'll look at the important elements of a team, but first we should acknowledge the primary people-reason for creating a team, the feeling that "together we can move mountains," and the most welcome words a teammate can hear, "I've got your back."

Many activities don't require the attributes of teamwork, but it has been my experience that forming a group into a team pays sufficient dividends to make the effort worthwhile, but only if you know how to do it.

I've worked in a few places where the tenor is to advance your career by finding fault with others' work. At these places, people strive to be better, or at least to look better, than their co-workers. There is little or no teamwork.

Except for a few strongly led organizations, especially sports teams, I have not heard of or observed substantial development or change efforts succeeding in such an environment. Successful change demands that your people have learned to work together in spite of differences and disagreements. This is true throughout the organization, but it is most critical at the workgroup level.

I've worked in team building for almost forty years, with Olympic teams, professional sports teams, high school teams, work teams, even families, but I didn't truly understand the core elements of teams until I met Rudy Williams about ten years ago.

He taught me his Four-Part Teaming Model that helped me make sense of creating and sustaining a work-team, and it will do the same for you.

Learn more about the Four-Part Teaming Model at rudywilliams.com and by reading
Mistake-Proofing Leadership and/or *Transparent Management*.

First, a work-team has to have a unifying vision. What is it that *all of us* want to accomplish? Without this figurative and mutual pot of gold at the end of the rainbow, individuals will not and cannot become a team.

During a crisis, this is easy. We all work together to survive, or we stand together in the unemployment line. This situation is a no other choice necessity requiring little discussion and eliciting no dissent. And it is usually seen as temporary; either we weather this storm until the sun shines again or we fail and seek our fortunes elsewhere.

Leaders hope that when they introduce Lean Thinking during a crisis, the benefits of waste reduction will be so strong and obvious that going back to the norm will not be an attractive option. Unfortunately, this doesn't always happen.

Your first task for a high functioning work-team is to create a vision for the work-team.

A good vision makes the work compelling. If the work is compelling, then getting the work done better and easier also becomes compelling.

Don't worry about backsliding if the work-team has an emotionally engaging vision. People will want to work together if they understand that the goal is compelling for everyone.

Second, the Four-Part Model mandates that all team members enjoy a sense of membership on the team. I initially thought this was the easiest part of team building—just buy everyone a similar hat and call it good. This step turns out to be the most difficult for most managers.

The crux of the sense of membership part is that:
- Each member knows why he or she should be on the team.
- Each member knows why every other member should be on the team.

The challenge for managers is the responsibility to remove people who do not belong on the team. Most places, this is not done.

Team sports provide a useful analogy for this element. Would you keep a first baseman on your team who couldn't play first base? Of course not. Everyone knows what a first baseman should do, and everyone would see that your first baseman can't play the position. Co-workers always know who is doing the work and who isn't.

The cost is high if you retain a team member who cannot perform. You are sending the message that mediocrity is acceptable, that you don't care about the goal, that others' efforts are unappreciated, and that you are not invested in the individual and collective interests of your team members.

Personal accountability is part of this element of team building. Have each team member present what he or she brings to the team and will be responsible for contributing. Have each answer the question: "What is my unique contribution to the team?"

The third part of the Four-Part Teaming model is influence on the team. Each member needs to know that he or she should and will influence the team.

It is enlightening to note that spring practice is held every year for big league baseball players. These players have been playing the game for a decade or more and are the best at it in the world. Yet they practice being a team.

How team members interact is another critical element in Rudy's model. He advocates making formal team agreements that each member signs. When problems occur, as they always will, this document can be pulled out to offer guidance on what to do next.

Formally or not, identify how members should interact with each other, how to make decisions, how to handle disagreements, and how to uncover and resolve the head butting, the heart breaking and the ego bruising that working together can cause. If the organization has implemented tools like Crucial Conversations, this step is relatively easy to take.

Rudy also taught me the thumb method to make team decisions. Like most leaders, periodically during meetings I tended to ask, "How does everyone feel about . . ?" and get various murmurs of agreement. But, with the thumb method, we engage one of Lean Thinking's best tools, visual control.

Now when I ask, "What do you think?" I get mostly thumbs up, which means "You can count on me one hundred percent" and everyone can see that. I get a few sideways thumbs which means, "I have some concerns, but you can count on me one hundred percent," and everyone can see that too. Sometimes I get a thumbs down which means, "I have some reservations, let's talk some more," so we do. It's a great tool.

Accountability is also fostered in this third part.

The fourth part of the model addresses, "What's in it for me?" Rudy calls it "Personal Reward."

Once the goal is defined and members find it compelling and well worth their time and effort, and when everyone knows that the right people have joined and the rules of engagement are identified and endorsed, then we can talk about making sure the work is personally worthwhile.

If you know what people want, and they know that you know, and you can provide it, all is well. If what a person wants is impossible, either that person doesn't belong on the team or you'll have to find another equally suitable reward. Sometimes the personal reward is wrapped into the vision, but often an individual wants more, like an altered work schedule to enable going to school two nights a week. Personal rewards must be provided.

Do you need to form teams to succeed?

No.

Do you create a significant advantage by forming teams?

Unequivocally yes.

Are teams really necessary to successfully implement Lean Thinking?

I'm surprised you had to ask.

○

Vision

I've worked with companies that did not have a vision statement and, of course, worked for a few whose vision statement I could never remember.

One healthcare organization where I worked had the vision to "be the quality leader." What else would they want to be, the second best? It wasn't until they later added the phrase, "and to transform healthcare" that I was emotionally engaged in the corporate definition of the future.

Managers seem to think that creating a vision takes too much time for little practical return in their investment. This is where the people side of Lean can confuse those interested only in process improvement.

Remember, Lean Thinking is identifying waste and eliminating it. Is there waste in taking time out from the work so a team can create a vision? In one way, yes. A customer would not pay for a work team to gather together and create a vision; the effort is total waste from the paying customer's point of view.

Employees are customers.

Employees will reward the effort to create a vision by being emotionally engaged with the work and with supporting one another, working hard and improving work processes.

A good vision:
   • Defines clear work unit objectives

- Promotes better decision-making
- Enables better teamwork
- Creates higher and more focused motivation
- Improves staff satisfaction
- Results in better outcomes
- Ends up with better financials

Ohno talks about processing as one area of probable waste. Doing the work of creating a team vision is certainly a lot of processing. To an enlightened leader, such an activity is, at worst, a necessary waste because we don't have a better way of initially creating a team. Usually however, the visioning activity itself is a value-added activity and outcome for team members and will benefit the organization as a whole and thus, all of its customers.

O

The Value Stream

The value stream is a tool to identify waste and thus prompt people to perform their jobs better. It also can be used as a method to enable workers to fully understand the value that they contribute.

Get your team together and talk about, "How our work creates value for our customers" in whatever way works for your team's roles. The objective is to help everyone understand each step of the process, the importance of every individual's contribution, how each step serves the customer and how interdependent the entire process is. Your team probably has multiple value streams. Take an interesting, damaged and/or critical value stream and look at all the activities, from the beginning to the delivery of the downstream product.

At this stage, do not overfill the steps of the value stream with data. Describing the activity, amount of time it takes, and how customer (including co-worker) value is added is sufficient at the beginning.

Get the team together and create a value stream that identifies on paper what each person does.

This will further solidify the membership portion of the Four-Part Teaming Model and introduce the concept of adding value along the value stream.

Discuss how to define value from the customers' and the employees' points of view. How is this value measured, monitored, improved? What happens when a problem arises?

Additionally, discuss how to handle potential problem areas. For car assembly, "stop the line" is exactly that— when a problem is noticed and can't be fixed quickly. The person that first notices the problem pulls a cord to either alert others or to actually stop the assembly line. The same thing happens during surgery or on an airplane flight deck. Do not allow a problem to proceed.

Talk about how to enhance value. How can quality be improved? Shall we speed things up? Is there waste in various steps? Are we using resources as well as we can?

This line of questioning begins the search for waste and the innovations of process improvement.

As needed, you could introduce other tools to help understand the value stream. For example, are materials collected a week or two before needed? It might be useful to talk about just-in-time or even the concept of takt time. Maybe a spaghetti chart would help identify waste. The point is not to teach tools, but to understand the value stream, how it can be used to improve quality, how it contains waste and that team members can significantly improve their work.

Tools will be learned as they are needed and used to identify the value of the work being done. Additional and more specific data such as percent value added can be measured as needed.

Discuss the benefit of meeting together to monitor the value stream. Would it help to huddle briefly at the beginning of the day to go over the schedule or perhaps at the end of the day to resolve any residual issues? Perhaps a weekly meeting would be enough.

While you're looking at the value stream from the perspective of the paying customer, look at it from the view of the employee. One of my favorite questions to ask is: What dumb things are we doing? Once people get into this mode of thinking, this question is a never-ending source of fruitful challenges.

Create a team highly invested in the compelling task of producing the absolute best value stream possible—and of continuing to improve it.

○

Team Leadership

The team leader has one primary function, *to do whatever is necessary to support team members in enhancing the value stream.*

The standard work for such leaders is receiving continual feedback from their primary customer-- employees.

These factors should guide every leader's decision: What is in the customers' best interest, what is in the employees' best interest, what adds value to the value stream and what eliminates waste from the value stream. Employees should know and trust that these are the leader's guiding principles.

When implementing Lean Thinking, 5S is one of the first and basic steps to organize the workplace. Often this involves cleaning up the area, like getting rid of family photos, souvenirs from past vacations, and a supply of thirty pens stuffed into a gnome-shaped penholder. A standardized workplace might be defined as having a maximum of three personal photos, no vacation souvenirs and three pens. Most often, these are arbitrary numbers decided by a committee up on the third floor.

However, if we keep in mind the leader's primary function, our 5S decisions will be based on what is good for the customer, the employee and the value stream. A 5S discussion by the team is the best way for a leader to make good decisions and to introduce value added and waste as criteria for decision-making.

No change, including the shift to Lean Thinking, should be or appear to be arbitrary. Make decisions that reflect improvement in the value stream. If a change doesn't accomplish this, don't make the change.

Leaders must clearly advocate for the customer *and* the employee. Promoting one over the other is looking for trouble.

In my experience, dress codes are a classic example of standardization, personal needs and arbitrariness run amok. Committees often initiated and run by people who want to implement a dress code or uniforms, either ram their ideas through because it will be "more professional," enlist the aid of senior leadership who want the same thing, or decide, without truly measuring, that this is what customers want. Many employees resent this, and rightly so. It usually has nothing to do with the value stream.

You might currently be doing something similar within your policies and procedures. Often these are to make management easier or for legal and administrative needs, not to improve value for customers and employees.

Employees should know, and it should be constantly demonstrated, that the value stream is every leader's primary guide.

Your job as a team leader is to set the stage for change, specifically in our case, implementing Lean Thinking. You don't do that by teaching Lean Thinking. You set the stage for change by creating a high functioning team that values meeting the customer's needs and their own as well.

If one or more employees do not respect the importance of the value stream, they may not be right for your team. If care is taken in team building and defining the value stream to include both customers and employees, having an employee who does not agree will be rare.

Once employees learn and accept the opportunities demonstrated by the value stream, they will be motivated to use their experience and practical problem-solving skills to improve it, if you don't get in their way.

Too often companies overdo training, teach tools before they're needed and turn practical ideas into abstract concepts. People sit in a classroom with strangers rather than work with their team and view slides instead of practicing value stream enhancing skills.

Employees should discover what is important, instead of being told. Adult learners have well-defined needs and being guided like children is not one of them.

As described in the book, *Influencer,* you must help your team recognize the importance of their work and their ability both to do the work and to improve it. Then you mobilize the sources of influence, personal, social and structural. As these are brought into action, you can make sure that continued improvement is inevitable, with reinforcement from the ever-growing benefits to customers and employees.

Learn to make the word "compelling" (from the employees' point of view) one of your favorite words and one of your most frequent tasks.

As a leader, if you can't make the work compelling (in a positive way) what good are you?

A great tool to do this is Appreciative Inquiry. You can assemble your team, propose a plan and ask four questions:
1.   What are the benefits of this course of action?
2.   What are your concerns?
3.   What is necessary to be successful?
4.   What are we willing to do?

By doing this, you can create action plan after action plan, all directed toward improving the value stream.

I have been greatly affected by the faith and discipline of the men portrayed in Alfred, Lord Tennyson's poem "The Charge of the Light Brigade."

The poem includes the lines,

>   *Forward, the Light Brigade!*
>
>   *Was there a man dismay'd?*
>
>   *Not tho' the soldier knew*
>
>   *Someone had blunder'd:*
>
>   *Theirs not to make reply,*

Theirs not to reason why,

Theirs but to do and die:

This is exactly the kind of leadership and the kind of following we must eliminate.

○

Harnessing the Speed of Thought

I created this tool a few years ago to help individuals and groups solve problems. I had noticed that groups, especially committees made up of personnel from different work areas, often swirled around multiple points of view when discussing (not solving) problems. They tended to offer different perceptions of the problem, promoted various solution possibilities and often chose the solution by voting, as if finding the best solution was a popularity contest. What should have taken minutes took hours and often resulted in mediocre decisions.

Researchers have a good idea of why this happens. Eric Baum in his book *What is Thought?* presents the idea that the human brain applies simplifying templates to find a good-enough solution almost instantaneously—perhaps as an instinctual survival process where speed is critical.

Thus, what happens in a group is that its members quickly identify, debate about, and vote upon a few solutions. The fastest person to arrive at a solution, or perhaps the most persuasive in the group, drives the decision. One person's brain power rules.

Instead, with the right tool, we can slow this process and benefit from the collective wisdom of the group.

Harnessing the Speed of Thought® (HST) is a five-step process that slows down the problem-solving process so that all participants take each step together, agreeing on each step before moving on.

The steps are:
1. Identify the issue
2. Define the goal
3. List hurdles and concerns
4. List possible solutions
5. Choose the best solution

This tool gives everyone the chance to contribute to each step. One key is to define a mutual (and compelling) goal so all are working toward the same end. Another key is to ruthlessly identify hurdles so the people can identify the solution that best overcomes those hurdles.

With such a parallel thinking/problem solving tool, the mysterious and invisible activity of problem-solving is externalized and can be standardized through visual control simply by working on each step using a white board.

Lean Thinkers are instructed to:

Decide slowly—Act quickly

With a problem-solving tool like Harnessing the Speed of Thought, you can:

Decide quickly—Act quickly.

o

Worker/Student

Many companies make it a practice to hire education specialists who know about teaching adults and somehow expect lessons learned in the classroom or on the computer to transfer to the workplace run by a manager who has no idea how to support learning. This is a common mistake.

Learning requires a great deal of reinforcement, more than most managers realize. The place for this reinforcement is on the job. The manager is the key link to help employees truly learn new skills. Turning workers into worker/students is not easy, but it must happen, and it must be led by the workgroup leader.

If you employ education specialists, have them teach managers how to coach worker/students. What these specialists can do easily you can do too with some extra sweat, and it is useful for non-education specialist managers to learn how.

Here are some things to do:
- Define the need so that everyone can see the obvious, and not so obvious; and agree that this is the need.
- Define the desired outcome so everyone agrees that the goal must be achieved.
- Discuss how to achieve this goal.
- Do a bit of Appreciative Inquiry.
- Put together an education plan.
- Discuss and decide how it should be implemented and monitored.

- Discuss and decide how success will be celebrated.
- Assign responsibilities and accountabilities.
- Implement the plan.
- Discuss with the team and individuals how the plan is working.
- Identify successes.
- Celebrate progress and accomplishments.
- Identify additional successes and celebrate.
- Find other needs and keep going.

You don't need to grade anyone, but a skills map detailing how each member of the workgroup is developing certainly helps. Such a map can easily be made in a grid. The left-hand column can contain employee names and the top row can describe the desired skills. You don't even have to identify anyone; a code number is fine.

Help employees understand what is important to learn, the best ways to learn and how to make it happen. Reinforce personal responsibility as much as possible and publicize how this learning and developing is improving the work and reaching important goals.

o

Prepare the People
Workgroup Checklist

Each member of the team knows why he/she is necessary and valuable to the team. ☐

Every member knows why every other member is important to the team. ☐

Every member knows why the leader is important to the team. ☐

The team has a compelling goal. ☐

The team uses formal and informal ways to influence how the team functions. ☐

Team members give each other constant feedback. ☐

All members of the team have declared personal rewards for being on the team. ☐

The team is constantly trying to improve the various team value streams. ☐

The team is learning process improvement tools just-in-time. ☐

The team uses specific problem-solving tools. ☐

The team leader is receiving constant feedback and is making changes as needed. ☐

THE INDIVIDUAL

What can we infer from Ohno's statement?

> *We discovered that industry has to accept orders from each customer and make products that differ according to individual requirements.*

If we view employees as customers, we can infer the importance of meeting the individual requirements of our employees.

In preparing the people, you can do a poor job at the organizational level and still find some success. You must do a good job at the workgroup level and, if you want to keep valuable employees, you must also do a good job at the individual level.

We must never lose sight of the fact that the most effective teams are comprised of people who are giving up their individuality. They decided to invest in the task, offering their expertise, time and labor for the good of the group.

Unless you can demonstrate that you have the best interest of each employee in mind, they will feel they are disposable and act that way, especially in a poorly constructed Lean environment.

What's in It for Me?

Employees have a well-documented "wants" list, including being appreciated, being kept informed of company issues, having personal needs respected, security, good salary, etc.

The majority of employees want, consciously or unconsciously, for the boss to share their values. This mutuality creates a safe workplace and a willingness to make important commitments.

Commonly, a paycheck pays for an employee's time and for doing the basic job. That's it. Anything else has to be paid for in other ways. To get what you want, you must know what to give in return.

If employees are motivated by the company vision and feel as though they are valuable members of a team, you're already meeting much of what is personally rewarding for them. The next step is to ask, individually, what else they want from their job. If what they want is possible, then tie it to performance or outcome. Promise it, and you're done. If what the person wants is impossible or otherwise unreasonable, you need to confront that immediately.

However, if what they want is only semi-unreasonable, start the discussion to clarify needs and responsibilities.

Say your employee wants to leave an hour early every Friday so he can visit his girlfriend at a local college. Is that unreasonable or is it something you could accommodate if he is otherwise doing a good job?

Would making your decision be easier if leaving early on Fridays was one of his identified personal rewards and his teammates were willing to cover for him? Such decisions are best made in a team environment.

People are going to meet their important needs one way or another. It is a wise leader who understands that and further, can ensure that everyone wins.

A paycheck is only a small portion of the what's-in-it-for-me formula and the most obvious; it's often not the most important.

> Managers tend to measure employees on one continuum, doing the job well or poorly. Why not add a second? How fulfilled they are performing the job.

Do a little informal digging and connect with your staff constantly. Needs change and so must rewards. Maybe along with a skills map, you can prepare a needs-met map.

○

Big Picture

Most employees are oblivious to the trials of the board room. All they see are the closed mahogany doors, the luxury lunches rolled in on a cart, and the pronouncements from on high that disrupt their daily lives, usually in a way that confirms that leaders have no clue of the workers' point of view. Change efforts are significantly handicapped if this is the common perception.

Workers want to know what is going on. They don't want or need to know everything; they understand confidentiality, and they appreciate candor. They don't like hedging. They don't like inconsistency. You will lose them completely if you're dishonest.

Connect the dots for them often, from the big picture to the company picture to the workgroup picture all the way down to the individual snapshot—how does each individual fit in.

Most employees have never heard of a SWOT analysis (Strengths, Weaknesses, Opportunities and Threats). Teach them what it is and what it looks like for your organization.

Communication (meaning encouraging and receiving sufficient feedback for every pronouncement) should take place five to eight times more than you think is necessary, especially the feedback to you part.

o

Best Day vs. Perfection

Explain the concept of perfection (when waste is eliminated from a process so that all activities along the value stream create customer defined value) in the workgroup first and then individually.

Explain the concept by discussing these levels. I like to draw different colored lines on a whiteboard to show the relative relationships.

1. Start with a bad day. Nothing is going right, but everyone is trying.

2. Talk about the work getting done as usual every day. This means that everyone is doing the job without working too hard.

3. Next, talk about everyone having a best day; work flows, people are happy, things are going as well as they can. The work is easy and rewarding.

4. The next level is how the best people in the world would do the job. Discuss how such individuals raise the bar for the rest of us.

5. Even higher on the list would be the performance of those who shared best practices and continued to focus on making the work even better.

6. Last would be perfection, when everything worked as well as it possibly could.

Talk about your team reaching a level between five and six and what steps to take to get there.

What you want to achieve is the sense that workgroups operate unnecessarily between levels two and three. This is not good for the customer and not good for the employee.

Discussing these levels enables people to see how much easier and more effective their jobs can be by sharing ideas. This is another benefit of forming teams.

○

Personal Mission Statement

Every employee works from a personal mission statement. It is part of their personal reward and a portion of their compelling task.

I have a few personal mission statements depending on what I'm doing. One is to *enable leaders to become the kind of leaders the world needs them to be.* This makes me feel as if I'm contributing to the world, which gives my life and work value.

One mission statement an employee of mine had was *to work just hard enough to keep my job so I can party on weekends.* He lasted a number of years with me because I knew what his mission was, and I kept him doing the tasks that needed to be done. He did the work I assigned him in order to keep getting what he wanted.

Many of your employees will not be able to articulate a mission statement. You can generate a generic mission statement as a team and individualize them as time goes on. The exercise itself is instructive.

Learn what each personal mission statement is, help fulfill it and keep track of your progress. Doing this can enable each of your employees to feel special and respected, a powerful combination.

○

Leading from the Middle

A good leader doesn't need to know the best answers, just the best questions.

A good heuristic is that if you're not regularly and pleasantly surprised by most of your employees, you're probably officious, rigid, regimented, authoritarian, distant and/or aloof. If you want to implement Lean Thinking, you can't be any of these (unless, or course, you're a revered, old-guard Japanese Sensei).

Each employee must feel encouraged to contribute. This means no set-in-stone process expectations. That's why you created a culture of innovation. Don't direct. Inspire. Let the ideas fly. Try things out. Fail forward fast.

All the Lean Senseis I have worked with are of one voice: *enable people to learn*.

The more directed employees are, the less they will invest emotionally. Find a balance between setting the direction and pace and allowing people to experiment to find better ways to achieve better outcomes than you could ever dream of.

Use Stephen Covey's delegation model outlined on the next page and learn what works best for each employee. Minimize rules as much as possible. And keep pushing yourself to allow more and more autonomy.

Covey: 1. Desired results 2. Guidelines 3. Resources
4. Accountabilities 5. Consequences

Knowing exactly what is expected is a confident
way of getting the work done and a good way of
mistake-proofing human behavior.

It isn't easy for a leader to let go. After all, leaders have a
great deal of responsibility. Most leaders have earned
their role with applied intelligence and hard work.
However, this doesn't mean the leader has to do it all
and it doesn't mean that the leader must control
everything.

A good leader leads—namely, informs everyone what
the goal is. After that, a good leader motivates. Pushing
isn't effective motivating. You hear a lot these days that
you can't make someone do something. That isn't true.
Facing the angry end of a gun motivates people to do a
lot of things. So does the need of a paycheck, until
something better comes along.

Working with individual people is exactly that, working
with individuals. Discover what makes each of them
tick, know their likes and dislikes, make them an
important part of the team, and of course, be stunningly
clear about company and customer needs and
expectations.

○

Emotional Engagement

This is the golden ring of employees performing the work and improving how the work is done. Helping employees become emotionally engaged is not difficult, but it doesn't keep forever. People change, their needs change, the situation changes. But for a while, often a long while, employees can be as loyal to the job as anything else in life.

We've covered much of it already. Create a trusting and supportive environment, ensure a sense of belonging and contribution, and make sure values are aligned.

Most important, connect to employees as individuals. People who are loyal are people who care. And what are they going to care more about, a process that is improved 22 percent or a fellow human being? What stirs more passion in a person, shaving 15 seconds off lead time or being sincerely thanked at the end of the day?

People do not work their fingers to the bone for a product, but for a sense of pride in that product, an emotion. You stir emotions with emotion, not data, policies or even your absolute best PowerPoint presentation.

Too many managers believe that it's necessary to create emotional distance from employees. This may be the norm in an authoritarian environment, but not one where you want individual employees to own the value streams and drive for improving processes.

People also cannot leave their personal troubles at the door. It just doesn't happen. If you expect it to or demand that it does, 150 years of science say it ain't gonna happen.

What is the easiest way to engage employees? Care about your employees. Show them that you care and will continue to learn how best to do that for each one.

The 4Cs of service (from *Earn Their Loyalty*) are helpful as a model for effective management:
1. Connect human-to-human 2. Collaborate
3. Contribute 4. Confirm satisfaction.

See Resources

You can even ask, "How can I help your work to be more fulfilling?" It will take a while to get all the answers. Trust takes time but start the process now and make sure to continue to get their feedback on how well you're meeting their needs.

o

Team Membership

Having a sense of belonging may be one of the prime human experiences and it seems to me that everyone seeks and benefits from such a feeling.

For an employee, working for an organization that is highly regarded in the community is a great start (*The Baptist Health Care Journey to Excellence* in Resources has many practical ideas for effectively and publicly promoting employees). Being a member of a highly regarded and successful workgroup is also rewarding. A topper on the sense of belonging is being individually thanked for specific contributions made.

Knowing why one is on a team is critical, yet this becomes a negative if feedback is rarely given or is insincere. I had one boss who ended our meetings together with a tossed off, "Keep up the good work." He ended his full department meetings the same way. I was quite sure he didn't understand my work and maybe didn't care. It would have been rewarding had he singled out one especially good effort, praised how much of a contribution it was, and then reverted to his catch phrase, but he never did.

Tell your people individually how well they are contributing to the value stream. Make your comments specific. And do it often. I don't know if this can be done too much.

○

Performance Reviews

I never saw the value of annual performance reviews and still don't, except maybe as an HR or legal requirement. Even then, performance reviews can be and should be significantly enhanced.

In a well-run organization, annual reviews should hold no surprises, so why bother? Planning and assessments should be performed regularly; you're creating a learning team that shouldn't wait a year for assignments, rewards, changes, new roles, training, agreements or anything else.

Do not manage by abstracts like a calendar, but by the needs of your people. You wouldn't delay needed maintenance on a machine simply because it wasn't yet due, so do the same for your people, and make it a joint review. (See Samuel Colbert in Resources for ideas to eliminate performance reviews.)

Make sure your reviews include organization, team and individual needs in equal proportion. Reflect on your role as a manager and how you and your employee contributed to each other's welfare. Discuss how each of you created new and better ways of getting the work done and revisit the vision statement and update your employee's mission statement. If you're after *continuous* improvement, how often do you think that you should review performance?

○

Work/Life Balance

If you're managing well, work/life balance is almost a non-issue. Work itself can be highly rewarding and stimulating. Frequent enough rewards and formal and informal celebrations of success are engaging and relaxing. Work can be as fulfilling and enjoyable as the best vacation.

Support two elements of the life part: Life outside of work and life that intrudes into work.

I rely on a study of the top ten employee "wants list" done years ago by the U.S. government, which found that number three on the list was help with personal issues (after appreciation and being kept informed about company issues). Be kind to the human beings who come to work everyday.

And encourage them to forget about work much of the time when they're home. They will be thinking about work anyway.

Caring about your employees isn't any different than routine maintenance on a machine, except it's easier to overlook and harder to do well.

Remember that work/life balance is different for everyone and may change from time to time.

○

Prepare the People
Individual Checklist

Someone in authority knows the employee's
mission statement and is doing what is
necessary to help the employee fulfill it.   ☐

Employees report that they are receiving their
identified personal rewards.   ☐

Each employee can accurately declare why he
or she is on the team.   ☐

Every employee reports an interest in moving
toward perfection by identifying and
eliminating NL activities.   ☐

Every employee works with teammates on the
value stream to create greater value.   ☐

Each employee enjoys a sense of belonging.   ☐

Each employee reports a rewarding work/life
balance.   ☐

Prepare the People Leadership Checklist

If you are going to lead a change or be involved in a change like implementing Lean Thinking, you will have to do some changing too. This listing will cover areas you should take into account as you move forward.

	Yes
Are you hiring the right people?	☐
Do you know how to hire the right people?	☐
Do you accept your own shortcomings?	☐
Are these shortcomings public?	☐
Are you working on the shortcomings?	☐
Do leaders have standard work?	☐
Can you let go of control?	☐
Are you an expert change agent?	☐
Can you and do you discipline without using power or threat?	☐
Do you create clear goals?	☐
Are you emotionally engaging?	☐
Do you match skills with the job?	☐

Do people know how to do the job well before you put them into the job? ☐

Do you ask for advice from your people? ☐

Do you encourage, even reward chance taking? ☐

Do you respond effectively to failure? ☐

Do you carve out time and otherwise support training for your people? ☐

Do you form high-performing teams (as opposed to workgroups)? ☐

Do you know what motivates adults? ☐

How are you doing so far?

Prepare the People Conclusion

Luckily, you don't have to be an expert in anything to successfully implement big changes, especially Lean Thinking. If I had to come up with one word to conceptualize what you must be, I'd say "sincere."

Leaders must be sincere in their quest to provide the absolute best value for customers; that is, people who pay you and the people you pay. If you truly believe that and keep that as your unwavering goal, you should be okay.

Toyota talks about meeting the needs of *individual* customers. Do the same for both of your customer groups.

It should come as no surprise that employees, like any other living organism, should be fully prepared for the demands they will face, especially change.

Provide employees with an environment that is safe, encouraging, clear, rewarding and engaging. If you didn't know how to do this before, you know now.

RESPECT THE
PEOPLE

You may have seen something like this: A slew of efficiency experts charges into a work area telling people to ignore them and to just go about their tasks. They incessantly click their stopwatches and scribble notes on clipboards for an hour or so before wordlessly disappearing. At best, people would be told their jobs were not in jeopardy (like anyone would believe that).

Process improvement often steps on the backs, the hands and the self-esteem of the people doing the work. You're not going to do that.

For much of its history, Toyota's knowledge base had been passed down orally. About ten years ago, senior executives compiled anecdotes, corporate wisdom and other statements into *Toyota Way 2001* and declared that Toyota's success rests on two pillars, continuous improvement and respect for people.

> (Respect for people) reflects respect for and sensitivity to morale, not making people do wasteful work, real teamwork, mentoring to develop skillful people, humanizing the work and environment...and philosophical integrity among the management team.
> Craig Larman and Bas Vodde
> *The Lean Primer*

Earlier, we noted Ohno's emphasis upon two pillars, just-in-time and autonomation. The reason for this book is the two new pillars of continuous improvement and respect for people, to ensure we are doing both in the right balance, in the right sequence and in the right way. I believe respect for people has been neglected.

In this section, we will look at leadership and a representative sample of Lean concepts along with the ways in which they can affect the respect for people pillar.

The danger of change, especially one as detailed and extensive as Lean Thinking, is inadvertently angering, insulting, embarrassing, hobbling, confusing and otherwise making your employees miserable, even your most resilient ones.

I have seen how continuous improvement can be introduced well, and I have seen how good ideas can go sour. I have watched hard-working employees stew for a few months as 5S and value streams were rolled out, mumble their concerns to a few close friends and eventually, sadly, quit their jobs. They didn't stay because they were convinced that their individuality would be erased by standard work. They feared their job satisfaction would be washed away by efficiency experts. They didn't want to be timed. They didn't want other people, who didn't do their jobs, telling them how to perform them. They resented being told their jobs were mostly waste.

And perhaps most importantly, they couldn't trust what was happening and didn't believe their voices would be heard.

Can you blame them? Everyone loses unless respect for people is emphasized as much (and probably more) as continuous improvement.

In this section we will identify areas where mistakes can easily be made and learn how to avoid them.

Lean

People Error: Assuming the word "Lean" means
                     something positive to employees.

Leaders think the word means more satisfied customers, higher efficiency, greater market share, better returns on investment and, last but maybe not least, a happier workforce.

What "Lean" means to many employees is working harder with fewer resources to produce more output in a draconian environment of constant harassment.

At the first hint of Lean, employees will Google and Wiki, talk with each other and perhaps ask a manager or two, who will shrug their shoulders and reply that they're not sure what it means. When paranoia fills the information vacuum, employees will begin to panic and start circling the help-wanted ads.

Most employees grow content in their jobs. They know what to expect and have in place ready-made responses to difficult situations. They know what works and doesn't work.

"Lean" means nothing will ever be the same again. Employees do not see that as a good thing. That's why you begin respecting the people by *preparing* the people.

o

Lean Leadership

People Error: Leadership doesn't have to drastically change to become effective Lean leaders.

Our working assumption is that a leader who is creating waste is going to be less successful than a leader who is not creating waste.

If you want your employees to doggedly seek out and eliminate waste, lead by example by doing the same yourself, to your leadership.

Picture yourself as a worker on an assembly line, but what you are assembling is not cars, but your employees. What should you be doing to perform to the best of your ability as each employee rolls by?

Here are a few ideas:
- Improve your management skills.
- Develop your employees.
- Be available as needed.
- Help eliminate their obstacles.
- Reduce fear and anxieties.
- Continually improve relationships.
- Reward effort.
- Ask Socratic questions.
- Apply Lean principles to your work.
- Contribute value each day to each of your employees.

It helps to gather a few other leaders, form a learning team, learn new models and methods and then experiment to discover the best standard work for managing the people side of change.

Another way of enhancing your respect for people leadership is to apply the five Lean principles (from Womack and Jones, *Lean Thinking*) to your management. Ask yourself:

Value: How much would employees pay me for my management work?

Value Stream: How am I eliminating NL behavior from my management work?

Flow: Am I interfering with or supporting my staff?

Pull: Am I available to those who need me?

Perfection: Am I applying poka-yoke, self-checks and successive checks to my leadership?

Leaders must be transparent. Just as visual control is a sine qua non of Lean Thinking, so must transparent management be for Lean leaders. Leaders must use management tools that are as near to poka-yoke as possible, tools that are clear enough to enable self-check and transparent enough for all employees to provide successive-checks.

Here are a few of the self-check questions a Lean Leader should ask:
- What am I doing to lessen the burden on my staff?

- What value-added behavior did I add today?
- How did I enhance trust?
- What did I help my staff learn this week?
- What am I doing to foster innovation?
- Am I applying autonomation well enough?
- What NL activities did I eliminate today?
- What did I do to improve my fat: lean behavior ratio?

Leaders should learn how to be good coaches; not in classrooms or by studying, but by participating in coaching labs and on-the-job training, just like their employees. The goal is to learn how to bring out the best thinking of your employees, not to teach them the answers.

Push-back must be welcomed, even celebrated, with leadership egos invested not in prestige, advancement or personal accomplishments, but in team spirit and team development.

○

Value

People Error: Telling employees at the onset that
much of their work is not value
added.

Employees have been trained how to do the work. They are doing the best they can. Don't begin process improvement with statements that their work is not value added. What they hear is that the work they have been doing is stupid and they probably are stupid too for not realizing it—and maybe stupid enough to be fired.

The way to approach value is to discuss what value truly is from the customers' perspective and identify what can be done to enhance that value. Identify a few areas, like the time it takes to respond to an order for example and explore how to *improve* value.

Along with this discussion, look at what employees value about the process. Walking down the hallway to a distant copy machine may take a few waste-creating minutes, but, "It sure feels good to get away from my desk and stretch a little bit." Acknowledge that benefit (and also the health benefit of moving away from the desk).

One unfortunate consequence of Lean activities to eliminate waste is the unintended elimination of what has value for employees. This is one way employees learn to define Lean as a negative.

It is critical to recognize that what may have no value for the customer may have significant value for the employee. This conflict of value should always be sought out, recognized and respected.

You should not build better processes from the sacrifices of your people, but from their ideas and actions. Improve quickly, but not faster than your employees can respond comfortably.

Help employees discover, from the actual work they do, the concepts of value added, non-value added but necessary, and non-value added, from both the customers' perspective and their own (using our convention of L and NL activities as appropriate).

As employees discover what is truly important, they will build on the concept of value and enthusiastically identify and eradicate waste wherever they see it, including in their own jobs.

O

Value Stream

People Error: Individuals are responsible only for their part of the value stream.

Toyota emphasizes teamwork—so should you. The workgroup owns the entire value stream; the individuals doing the work on portions of the value stream do not own their particular parts.

A challenge for most companies implementing Lean Thinking is what to do when jobs change or are eliminated. If the entire team owns the value stream, individuals can move from one part of the value stream to another and still enjoy a sense of pride and ownership in the process.

Some experts place responsibility for improving the value stream on management because this level can more easily see and monitor the entire process. Leaving it at this level, however, is a mistake. The more workers can utilize the big picture (ending with the customer), the better. This gives them an increased sense of contribution to the work and to the end result.

○

Identifying Waste

People Error: Identifying waste only from the
                     customer's perspective.

This is similar to defining value. I've seen a team of change experts measure a process and conclude that 97.8% of the work being done is waste. Any guess as to how that makes the workers feel? Is how they feel important?

The people that are told that 97.8% of their work is waste automatically think that 97.8% of their job will either be eliminated or changed in yet unknown, but probably unpleasant ways.

A good way to start the waste conversation is to ask, "What doesn't seem right about your job?" This will not necessarily be from the customer's perspective, but it will get the waste ball rolling. Then figure out ways to identify the irritating stuff. Does the work take a long time to do? Is it confusing? Are the results worth the effort? Is the work necessary at all? Develop your own tools to identify waste. This is what Toyota did over a number of years. The process of inventing or learning tools itself adds value to implementing Lean Thinking.

After you begin measuring waste with your homegrown tools from your employees' point of view, add the paying customer's point of view in meaningful ways.

o

Perfection

People Error: Defining perfection as the target
while saying it is impossible to reach.

If people are told that perfection is the goal, but that it is impossible, they will rightly think that management has not quite thought this one through. They will then mistrust much of what else is said.

Instead, people should be told that perfection is the goal and we simply don't know enough at the moment to reach it. But we will know enough eventually. Define it in small bites. Have we been perfect? When? Can we be perfect for fifteen minutes? If we can do that, how about doing it for an entire morning?

Also ask: What will be different when we are perfect? Can we achieve some of that now?

Perfection has different faces. A completely satisfied customer who paid the lowest price for the highest quality is perfection. An employee who reports a satisfying day of excellent work is perfection. A boss thanked by employees for effective leadership is perfection.

Enjoy the idea of perfection. Talk about it. Make it real rather than an elusive and impossible to reach abstraction.

○

5S

People Error: Making 5S policy driven rather than customer driven.

Employees, especially desk-jockeys, hate it when people from other places in the company tell them what to do. They also dislike the boss making arbitrary decisions that affect the comfort and control of the workplace.

I've observed heated debates over how many personal photos should be allowed on a desk. If a mysterious committee defines the maximum as three, someone asks if a family collage in only one frame counts as one.

Doing a work area 5S should include the actual workers and if possible, someone who can *coach* 5S. The guiding principle should be "What is in the best interest of our customer?" and making sure both types of customers are included. Make your best decisions and see what works.

As 5S is often the start of a Lean Thinking effort, examine the ramifications on employees.

The first S, Sorting, is beneficial to the company to reduce waste, especially of excess inventory. For the employee, Sorting means risking not having necessary supplies on hand. This is where arbitrary decisions can set the wrong tone for all those yet to come.

Simplifying for the company keeps the workplace neat and improves inventory control. But for the employee,

Simplifying means promoting an industrial look, giving up control and perhaps actually decreasing efficiency.

Sweeping helps the company with holding the gains and accountability. For the employee this can mean extra work, and perhaps an IBM-type of sterile, uniform, corporate atmosphere.

The fourth S, Standardizing, promotes a focus on best practices and enables easier people and process substitutions and continuous improvement. Employees can lose a sense of independence and self-reliance, making the work mind-numbingly routine.

Self-discipline leads to sustainability, but for the employee; this means that things will never get back to normal and new tasks are just more work without more pay.

To overcome these differences in perception:
- Acknowledge the different benefits, company/employee.
- Make sure personal gains are identified.
- Include staff in all 5S work.
- Teach that 5S is a process, not all or none.
- Always base 5S decisions on what is best for the customer.

Remember that 5S is simply another tool and not an end in itself.

○

Just-In-Time

People Error: Promoting just-in-time too much or too soon.

Just-in-time is critical to eliminate waste, to reduce processing and costs and to improve quality. It lowers the water so the rocks (wastes) are exposed. Striving for just-in-time makes it easier to identify waste and eliminate it.

However, when workers are told they will have to operate from an inventory that is provided just-in-time, they become anxious. They know that shortages will cause all sorts of problems and anticipate that their jobs will be a mess.

Employees should be helped to understand that just-in-time will happen over time and that inventories will decrease only as the ability to be in flow increases.

Like most of the other topics in this section, employee misperceptions and fears about Lean Thinking must be acknowledged and respected. They will not go away just from training and they will certainly not go away because you say they should.

As you would do for any identified waste, you should uncover any misperceptions and fears and do whatever it takes to eliminate these thoughts and feelings. Usually all this requires is listening.

○

Standard Work

People Error: Promoting standard work as what
everyone must do.

For Ohno, standard work has three components:
1. Cycle time
2. Work sequence
3. Standard inventory

Organizations tend to broaden the term to mean the way everyone is supposed to perform. For example, standard work may be to rearrange the tables and chairs a certain way when leaving a meeting room. The concept has decayed from a specific tool designed to promote assembly line efficiency to a tool promoting uniform behavior. Standard work has become an outcome rather than a tool.

People fear the loss of individuality and creativity. Some of a company's best employees are the first to escape to other companies where they will be more appreciated.

> Rigid standards make monitoring easier:
> They inhibit kaizen

Standard work is just a tool, an important one to enable improvement in effective and measured ways. If everyone did the job any which way, it would be difficult to know what to improve.

I like to help employees understand the concept as "best practice." Let's discover together the best way to get the job done, everyone working in the best way, and we'll continue to improve from there.

Henry Ford said standards should come from people doing the work, not from someone at the top.

The idea of standard work is not a fixed practice; the definition of standard is only a starting point for further improvement. Knowledge is widely shared, not mandated. Allow individual workgroups to decide how to implement the standard and how to improve it.

In most situations, standard work should be defined locally by the workgroup and then shared with everyone.

○

Mistake-Proofing

People Error: People think they must avoid making
mistakes.

Often employees are not aware of the difference
between a mistake and a defect (a problem affecting the
customer). Quite a few believe that Lean Thinking is
supposed to eliminate every mistake, a discomforting
expectation for any normal human being.

Help employees realize that making mistakes is an
acceptable part of becoming Lean. The mantra should
be: "Let's try it. The worst that can happen is we're
wrong."

As this approach is sinking in, help employees
understand that unstable systems that allow variation
cause most mistakes. Employees are doing their best. If
something goes wrong, the idea is to determine the root
cause and fix that, not to criticize the worker. This is
where your work with Just Culture is important.

Understand errors more; punish less. Focus on the tools
of mistake-proofing, standard work (or best practices),
poka-yoke, self-check and successive-check as the best
ways of ensuring a mistake does not become a defect.

o

Ippon Seoinage*, Etc.

People Error: Making Lean tools too complicated
                 and foreign.

Coping with new terms and concepts can be confusing, especially if using a Japanese vocabulary. (A substantial minority of employees are critical of not using perfectly good American words.) It is a mistake to force-feed alien concepts and words. Keep things simple.

Avoid the confusion and resentment trap by remembering that Lean tools are tools, not ends in themselves. If a tool doesn't fit well in a situation, don't use it. If a native tongue word is better, use it. Honor people more, jargon less.

At the same time, new terms can be highly beneficial. For example, when a mistake occurs, it is far better to say, "Let's find the root cause" than the more common, "Whose fault is this?"

Take all the time you need to introduce Lean concepts and tools in ways that make sense to your employees. Do not make learning Lean into a language class or a culture clash.

o

---

* Ippon Seoinage is a judo throw.

RPIW and Kaizen

People Error: Leaders choose process issues to
address with only rare inclusion of
people development.

Organizations use RPIWs and Kaizen events as
structured ways of making improvements that can be
publicized to further the Lean Thinking effort. However,
too much structure can suppress motivation and
creativity. Make sure these happen:
- Home and away teams understand and
value the importance of the change effort.
- They agree to the defined outcomes.
- They have the ability to influence the work
and the outcomes.
- They are aware how customers and
employees will benefit from the outcome.

Rudy Williams' Four-Part Teaming model is an absolute
best practice to form an RPIW or Kaizen team, especially
if the compelling task focuses on increasing customer
value and the deliverables include developing the
participants. It can take only 30 to 45 minutes to form a
team and is well worth the time.

You can also use De Bono's six thinking hats exercise
with these "hats" for the people doing the change work:
- Yellow—What do we like about this change
effort?
- Black (or purple)—What barriers are there?
- White—What are the facts?
- Red—How do we feel about this effort?

You should also measure how well you are creating change agents. After an RPIW, Kaizen or other structured improvement effort, ask participants these kinds of questions and report the results:

- What made this a significant problem?
- How were you emotionally engaged in the change effort?
- What is your motivation to keep the gains?
- How engaged was the home team?
- What made this experience valuable?
- What did you learn?

Asking these and similar questions, then using the answers to improve the process and also reporting people development results to the organization are critical for respecting the people.

> The more kaizen is directed from the top, the less kaizen you have.

The ultimate goal is for every employee to be an active change agent. Becoming one requires the employee to overcome one entrenched habit, doing the job as instructed. Minimize the instructions on how to accomplish kaizen.

Another good way of overcoming this habit is to ask the team and individual workers Socratic questions, such as what should we change to improve the work? Ask every day. Compile efforts and results. Reward participation. Reward chance taking. Reward change.

The ultimate goal would look like this: A supervisor about to chat with an employee is interrupted by another employee who says, "Boss, I was just doing a little experiment and learned that if we move the workbench two feet to the left, it is easier and safer to reach the tools and we can save maybe five seconds every cycle."

Kaizen is the continuous effort of breaking down processes and putting together a more harmonious whole. The new may or may not resemble the old. This also includes the kaizen process. Don't be afraid of allowing employees to discover new ways to discover.

Let go. Perfection cannot be achieved by simply polishing the old ways, especially old leadership ways.

○

Training

People Error: Training is done in
                    convenient groupings.

A common tactic is to schedule training during the workday in ways that won't disrupt production. This usually means that a few members from each workgroup attend training with people from other workgroups. Often this training is not just-in-time for job performance but covers the fundamental concepts everyone should know and be aware of. Equally often, these concepts are not applicable or applied in the workplace right away and are soon forgotten.

It is best to train a workgroup together so they can support and encourage each other and improve the work as a team.

Toyota emphasizes training. Ensure workers are able to do the job before they are on-the-job. Advanced training is often on-the-job or through simulations.

Training should be an expectation for every employee and should be a priority for the organization.

Train employees so they can do their job well and train them so they can teach you how the work can be done better. And tell every employee that this is your goal.

Training should not be defined as only formal instructor and student. Training is learning how to do things better. This can and should include putting co-workers together to examine the value stream and see what can be improved. It includes a staff member calling another to get ideas about how to improve a process. It includes an informal team of people doing similar work in separate places and connecting once in a while to compare notes.

Define training as learning how to improve value — in any way that may achieve that outcome.

Lean has resurrected the World War II era Training Within Industry concepts. With many workers leaving for the service, the War Department designed training for inexperienced workers to fill the void. The idea was to simplify and explain the work so trainees could succeed faster and more competently.

They made effective training a significant part of the war effort. This kind of thinking seems like a good idea now too.

○

Additional Areas

Change, and most notably rigorous change such as Lean Thinking, creates chaos. Some people will quit. Try not to lose the good ones. A few people will stay and openly or covertly complain or even sabotage the ideas and efforts of process improvement.

Others will be passive, working below the radar and hoping to keep their jobs with minimum interference. Another substantial minority will want to get with the program, but they won't because of inadequate training.

Often the thought is, "Sure, I'll be fine as long as it doesn't get too bad." What you want is for the great majority to say, "This is great, my work is so much better now."

A small point, but an important one that is almost always missed: Don't use industrial examples of Lean with knowledge workers. Find or create stories and examples that directly relate to their work.

Display efforts and gains so employees and customers can see them whenever possible.

William Bridges' *Transitions* makes a great point about change not being the problem so much as the emotional transitions that accompany it. Understand the dynamic of loss, the neutral zone and new beginnings.

If people have input into change and influence over the goals and how to reach them, transitions need not be a major hurdle.

Ohno's metaphor of baton passing is helpful in coping with individual differences. In a running relay race, the baton passing zone is long, so that the best runner can run the greater distance when the baton is handed off. Using this concept helps to ensure that work processes take into account the range of individual abilities.

Employees also must understand that their co-workers have a wide range of abilities. A person will contribute more one time than another time. Employees keep score on this, so you should monitor it as well.

Always be flexible, but equal in the long run.

Just as machines can be equipped with stopping devices when a problem occurs, make sure your employees are too. This may be inconvenient sometimes, but the value of ensuring that employees control the process and know they control it is not to be dismissed.

If the majority of your Lean training is via PowerPoint slides, you have seriously weakened your training and your employees' interest in reducing waste and adding value.

One last word on respecting the people.

Know how each employee defines what respect is and do your best to do that, just like you would for the paying customers.

o

Respect the People Checklist

Employees define "Lean" as a way to add value for all customers. ☐

Improving the value stream is a team effort. ☐

Employees own the value stream, not their jobs. ☐

Change and 5S are customer driven. ☐

Employees are providing frequent feedback. ☐

Standard work is defined at the lowest level. ☐

Standard work is defined locally. ☐

Information is shared globally. ☐

Lean tools are not goals. ☐

Kaizen is evolving from scheduled events to daily occurrences. ☐

No one leaves training or a meeting confused. ☐

Training is to specified levels of skill. ☐

Leaders are competent with "soft skills." ☐

Mistakes and unstable processes are frequently reported. ☐

Respect the People Conclusion

If you're like many leaders I have worked with, you are taken aback by the amount of effort it takes to create the right kind of environment for employees. It takes daily diligence (or put into Lean terms, a "daily management system").

Just as you want perfection in your processes, you should want perfection in leadership and management.

But it isn't as high a mountain or as steep a path as you may imagine.

Just as Lean Thinking is not the application of a set of tools, respecting the people is not something done to them from your vast store of knowledge, but with them, from their vast store of knowledge. That's why you hired them.

GROW THE PEOPLE

The assembly line is a beautiful metaphor for what we want to accomplish. We want everyone doing a good job, performing exactly as needed when needed to pass a defect-free product to the worker next in line and culminating with customers receiving exactly what they desire.

"Growing" the people means that as we improve processes, we improve people.

If we had a perfect process to grow employees, what would the product look like?

Here are a few considerations for the ideal employee:
- Has been trained to do the job
- Has a customer service mentality
- Knows who the customers are, what they want and how to meet their needs
- Is fulfilling a personal mission statement
- Is willing and able to give truthful feedback
- Ends most workdays highly satisfied

- Continues to learn
- Is a supportive teammate

Is your organization currently producing such valuable employees?

We want workers to be emotionally engaged in the work and to be on the constant lookout for ways to improve everything. Improving everything means improving value processes, relationships, problem solving, speed, errors, training, following, leading, communicating critiquing, *everything*.

The ultimate outcome of growing the people is employees examining process value streams and also examining people value streams; all the while creating testable improvements.

Having clearly defined goals for production and training and having easily observed progress displays enables employees to know what is expected, how they are doing and what to focus on.

Another way of looking at this is to recall perfection, the fifth principle of Lean, which is defined as the complete removal of all waste along the production value stream. The value stream we have been looking at is different; it's the one that produces a productive and engaged employee, one who is totally committed to using Lean Thinking and fulfilling personal potential.

Developing the right kind of leadership to manage the people side of lean requires a lot of effort. Let's look at the most important areas.

Performance

Obviously, high performance is the desired end result: everyone performing well and regularly improving his or her work and outcomes.

You may be familiar with this formula:

Performance = Ability x Motivation x Opportunity[*]

As a leader, your responsibility is to optimize all three. A good way to do this is to enlist the help of your employees. Explain the formula to them. Ask what can be done to enable everyone to do the best they can.

Put up a chart where employees can see it (for visual control) listing the important abilities people are working on, what motivates them (personal mission statement, company vision, anticipated bonus, etc.), what barriers inhibit them and what is being done to overcome the barriers.

For each element of the formula, you could have a separate listing. For ability, a skills chart is a proven way of documenting growth that itself is a great motivator.

Motivation could be measured by level of satisfaction at the end of the workday, emotional engagement for the current project, or level of interest in joining a

---

[*] See *Academy of Management Review*, 1980, Vol. 5 #3, Situational constraints and work outcomes: The influences of a frequently overlooked construct. Lawrence H. Peters and Edward J. O'Connor.

committee. Anything that spotlights motivation is useful.

For opportunity, a chart that identifies team problems and lists solutions and how well they are working does wonders for morale, even if the problems are resistant to solutions.

Performance reviews should be frequent (to ensure important current items to work on are identified) and with two parts: how the employee is meeting the organization's needs and how the organization is meeting the employee's needs. And, of course, don't design the performance evaluation form yourself (or use the generic one from HR if you don't have to) have your team do it. In addition, opportunities for training and other growth experiences can be listed and updated as to who is doing what to improve themselves. People love this kind of recognition.

○

Accountability

Accountability is fostered through:
- Intrinsic motivation
- Clearly defined expectations
- A team atmosphere

An authoritarian boss can often get compliance, but rarely commitment or accountability. When a stick motivates behavior, that stick always has to be in view out of the corner of an eye and also has to be swung every once in a while.

A true leader can foster commitment if the vision and the outcome of the work are compelling. A vision internalizes motivation if the employee understands and believes in the goal and, as a valuable member of a team, willingly accepts responsibility to make that outcome happen. The team element is important to move from blaming others for failures to investing with teammates to do whatever it takes to overcome problems.

If problems arise, it is human nature to point at the person or authority who declared how the work was to be done. If the employee agrees with the goal and has influence over how to reach it, motivation and accountability flourish.

A constraint is how well the team agrees on the tasks to be done. Even if there is agreement on the goal, there is often disagreement on how to achieve it. Like with the thumb method of group decision-making, if someone is uncertain, but is 100 percent committed, that works.

If someone has commitment reservations, those reservations have to be addressed and overcome or that person may not be right for the team. Reluctance and force are toxic for accountability.

○

Sustainability

Keeping change moving forward is like herding cats; hard to do by mere humans. Don't try. Have the cats herd themselves.

After a Herculean effort by management to change a process, it is commonly off to the next challenge while the new behavior slowly degrades into old habits. A lot of pulling, prodding and poking take place to support the new behaviors.

This is not the right focus. The way things are done is not the reason for the change. The outcome is the reason for the change. The benefit is not that a task takes 18 seconds less time, but that the outcome is achieved 18 seconds faster. Focus less on activities and more on how well the new outcome is being sustained and ask if this is the best we can do.

Some changes in how tasks are done are for safety or other critical reasons. Reverting to unsafe or ineffective behavior is not acceptable. But keep your eye on the outcome.

The more you focus on outcomes rather than activity, the easier it is to sustain change.

The British National Health Service (Lynne Maher et al, 2002) created a useful sustainability model that details important change factors to monitor.

Some of the questions to answer are:

- Does this change improve efficiency and make jobs easier?
- Does the change look right?
- Can the change be adopted elsewhere in the organization?
- Can the benefits be monitored and celebrated?
- Have staff and leadership been engaged in the process?
- Is the change in alignment with the organization's mission and goals?
- Has the change become part of the infrastructure?

The model is designed to enable an organization to score themselves on the identified factors important for sustainability.

Note that no one person is accountable for sustaining the change. Leaders are recognized for their level of commitment and influence, but otherwise, this approach emphasizes the benefits of the change and ensures everyone involved appreciates the benefits.

Again, it is the new outcomes and not the improved processes that are important. Process follows outcome. Cats head toward the food.

Describing the food and the route to get there is important. Lean Thinking tier three reporting is reporting to the board what is happening, tier two is sharing effort and outcomes with leadership and tier one is doing the same at the workgroup level.* At all

---

* Some places number tiers in the opposite sequence; tier three

levels, it is a mistake to report only process improvement.

Tier one reports are often weekly, when a workgroup gathers around a "vis wall" (easily viewed data of process improvement efforts and other measures of the work), to review how things are going.

A critical component of sustainability is employee engagement. One way to enhance that is to include "grow the people" data in all tier reports, e.g. who is attending training and how that is going. One third of the data should be how the organization is going, one third how the workgroup is contributing and one third how the people are doing.

These are necessary elements of a good tier one report:
- Stories of successes
- Communication about outcomes, including feedback and concerns
- Asking questions about the data, such as how can we do the work better
- Collect suggestions on how to improve the report

In addition, regular team huddles can help sustain sustainability. These are quick meetings before the day, in the middle of the work time or at the end. Huddles are designed to predict potential problems, to solve current ones or to share information to help get the work done.

---

being the worker level and some places also define 4 or 5 tiers.

Like a painting project, sustainability is in the prep work. Don't look for an after-the-change secret to keep it going.

The more you can align your forces before any change, the easier change will be. Start with great momentum and afterwards all you need to keep it going is a gentle nudge now and then. A good way to nudge is to ask an intriguing question like, "What do you think this will look like in six months?"

○

Leader Development

Organization development professionals have identified important components for improving the workplace. Here are a few:

- Systems integration
- Leadership strengths and weaknesses
- Relationships
- Trust levels
- Expectations
- Goals
- Problems and opportunities
- Values
- Power structure
- Corporate "culture"
- Policies and procedures

Being aware of these areas, measuring them, and improving them is part of growing the people. Our working assumption is that fifty-percent of each of these areas is fulminating with waste you cannot see but that everyone in the company can feel.

Improving these areas in a visible way is a basic leadership responsibility.

If you don't have an organization development department, consider hiring an OD consultant to help you evaluate these areas, especially if you are planning big changes like Lean Thinking.

Continuous improvement should not focus solely on processes, unless you include interpersonal behavior as a set of processes, which is exactly what we're doing, especially for leaders.

Leadership training should also be just-in-time and to a pre-defined level of competency. And like for everyone else, training should be well-practiced before being used on the job, which means simulations and labs.

What are we talking about?

How well do you discipline a good employee who has made a significant mistake? How well does everyone on the management team do it? Is there a standard process (best practice) that everyone uses? Does everyone use it to an accepted standard of competency? If your organization is like most, the answers to these questions will be unsettling. You must do something to improve that.

The people side of Lean Thinking mandates that you create a training system so that leaders can pick from and use the right leadership tools, mistake-proof their leadership and continually improve their leadership.

One method for leadership development is a mentoring program. Another highly effective approach is a set of collaborative sessions on selected topics where leaders learn a skill, practice it together and then try it in the workplace. They return to the collaborative to share their experiences, learn from each other and then move to the next skill.

Leadership development is critical to Lean Thinking, is wide-ranging, takes a significant degree of openness and consequent courage, and should be continuous and public.

A well-tuned leadership development program will supercharge growing the people.

○

Stories

Nothing engages people like a good story. You can either be the story, making your point while playing a guitar and wearing a ten-gallon hat, or tell the story in a way that makes people lean forward in their seats, wide-eyed and expectant, wondering what will come next.

I once chatted with a senior leader who was going to present telephone answer-time data to a large group of managers. She wanted to make her point with a phone ringing for 38 seconds before being answered. I reminded her to wait while tension built and not respond to her own tension. She did. In the midst of her presentation to a packed auditorium, she allowed the phone to ring for the full 38 seconds before reaching for it. She created dynamic tension and people talked about it for years.

Nordstrom is famous for once allowing the return of two snow tires even though they didn't sell tires. Although this may or not be true, it demonstrates the power of a story, one as short as just a few lines, to guide people to do the right thing. A good story is better than thirty-six pages in an employee manual. Even a bad story is worth more than twenty-two pages.

Telling a good story is relatively easy. You don't do the usual—tell people what you're going to tell them, tell them and then tell them what you told them. Instead, feel the story from your insides as you tell it and take your listeners up a winding trail to a heart-felt climax.

While studying writing, I learned one of the secrets of good fiction: Have the hero climb a tree to save a kitten, then build tension by throwing increasingly large rocks at him until the hero is almost dead. As he continues the struggle and is just in reach of the kitten, throw the biggest rock. Indiana Jones lives!

Drama sells. Conflict engages. Stories inspire.

Organizations are competing against a thousand highly engaging distractions every day. A good story will hold employees' attention and get them engaged.

Think about which leader you would stay late for, work weekends for, give your absolute best for—one that told you an inspiring story or one that presented a colorful and informative slide show. Which are you doing?

o

Feedback

Feedback is the verbal form of visual control. Feedback promotes flow and adds value. It is a vital part of mistake-proofing. It helps identify and overcome the natural contradictions of the Toyota Production System.

Development Dimensions International (DDI) has a useful tool/technique for feedback called the STAR method. It makes sense to employees and it works. STAR is an acronym that stands for Situation or Task, Action and Result.

I teach a tool called "Ob-Quest." It combines your observation of a situation with asking a relevant question. For example, "I think we aren't training the line staff to do the job quickly enough. Do you think it's our training or something else?" The discussion can then be about how others define the problem until the problem is agreed upon and solutions can be sought.

Here's another example. "Hey Harold, I'm not sure your presentation covered all the important data of the Wilson account. How do you see it?" Joe may see it differently.

People will get used to the idea that feedback is simply an observation that may or may not be accurate, but it is the beginning of sharing points of view.

More formally, feedback can be part of a people development continuum including feedback, coaching and mentoring. Feedback is given immediately to enable an employee to improve or to reinforce a good job. Coaching can be done with people over time to improve performance and to help them reach a predetermined goal. Mentoring is beneficial to high performers who can be supported over an extended time to fill important jobs.

○

Coaching

Coaching is a difficult skill for many leaders to acquire. It's vague and slow. Leaders tend to want to move quickly toward defined goals, reach those goals and immediately move on to the next set of goals. Coaching is frustratingly elusive to grasp and seemingly convoluted in the doing; it is much easier to direct than to guide.

However, coaching is a critical skill in helping employees become change agents. Being taught to see waste is one thing, discovering how to see it is an enriching experience and more likely to stick.

You develop leader/coaches the same way you coach; by helping them discover what coaching is, often through a coaching lab. The way this can work is for three leaders to form a learning team. They are given coaching material, including a list of desired coaching behaviors to study and discuss.

Over four to six coaching training sessions, using a standard scenario, the three leader/learners coach a trained coachee who responds positively when the coaching is done correctly and not so well when the coaching is done poorly. The two other learners observe and comment after each scenario. The learning by doing often results in an "aha" moment when the leaders understand the difference between directing, teaching and coaching. Participants learn how to help the coachee *discover* what is important.

Scenarios can include common situations such as forming an initial partnership with the coachee, dealing with someone who is stuck, giving feedback, coping with conflict or stress, disciplinary issues and reaching performance goals.

Important coaching behaviors to emphasize are being open and honest, taking risks, empathy, reflecting, linking coaching and performance, asking open-ended questions, providing emotional support and supporting self-discovery.

Becoming a good coach is not being taught how to do it but experiencing how to do it. Coaching in a simulation is safe; a post-discussion of what you did and why is enlightening; and observing others sweat and toil when it's their turn is both a relief and a revelation.

Coaching is one of the premier skills of a good Lean manager, but one that is often overlooked. A leader whose goal is to help staff fulfill potential must be an exemplary coach.

○

Grow the People Checklist

Employees are rarely, if ever, surprised. ☐

Managers are often pleasantly surprised by their staff. ☐

Employees accept accountability for value outcomes. ☐

Leaders are effective story tellers. ☐

Employees are providing more feedback than ever before. ☐

Employees report being in a "partnership" with their boss. ☐

Turnover is at historic lows. ☐

Growing the people is measured in effective, public and reinforcing ways. ☐

Employees repeat some of the great company stories. ☐

Sustaining change is easier than ever before. ☐

Employees give training high marks and request more training. ☐

Employee performance continually improves. ☐

Grow the People Conclusion

Toyota believes it will prevail in the marketplace through two major efforts, out learn and out develop the competition. You can do the same through growing the people.

You are doing an important part of your job if people are trained and motivated to continually improve what they do.

Management is responsible to enable employees to live the TPS principles (From *The Toyota Way*, Liker, 2004):
- Long term focus
- Work toward flow
- Use pull systems
- Level the work
- Stop and fix
- Standardize, then improve
- Visual controls
- Use short tests
- Grow leaders who teach
- Develop individual and teams
- Grow everyone on the value stream
- See for yourself
- Make decisions slowly by consensus; implement quickly
- Kaizen relentlessly

Your people are truly growing when all this (except maybe making decisions slowly) is happening.

MORE TO DO

More to do. More to do. Always more to do. This can quickly become a tedious refrain. As we discussed earlier, those who wish to lead a successful Lean Thinking change must be willing and able to change themselves, and make many of those changes public. And of course, all employees must be prepared and able to change too.

Change must become part of an organization's DNA, as common an expectation as arriving for work on time.

What this means for leadership is the constant reinforcement of change efforts, successful or not. Leaders must lead by example, walking the talk of failing forward fast and, at the same time, creating a culture where learning and growing is expected of everyone.

Our Lean goal in this case is defined as every step of implementing Lean Thinking advances both continuous improvement *and* respect for people.

Increasing value is the specific goal of continuous improvement while fulfilling human potential is the specific goal of respect for people.

When Leaders Make Mistakes

Our exploration of the people side of Lean opens a complex Pandora's Box of leadership responsibility and accountability. We expect line workers to call attention to a problem immediately, something they have caused perhaps or a difficulty that requires attention. We should expect no less from leadership.

Leaders must lead the effort toward mistake-proofing. This means leadership standard work is identified and followed. This also means leadership poka-yoke, self-check and successive check. Successive-check is the most important; employees must have the necessary support and encouragement to call attention to leaders' missteps.

A lot of good comes from leaders telling stories about recent gaffs and what they are doing to make up for errors and preventing them from happening again.

Behind the scenes, of course, the normal Just Culture response can deal with any disciplinary issues.

o

The Role of the Sensei

Hiring a sensei (teacher) of Lean Thinking is a wise decision. It means having an experienced guide on a difficult journey; that alone makes it worthwhile. But the idea is good for a lot of other reasons. One is that it symbolically assures that the company is serious in its quest for continuous improvement. Often a sensei is contracted for five years, further demonstrating strong commitment and awareness that this continuous improvement process takes time.

Equally important, often the sensei can help achieve radical improvement in a short time, proving that this new way works.

A Japanese sensei, especially one who does not speak English, adds a mysterious exotic flavor emphasizing that Lean Thinking is different. For some, this will be a negative: "Why do we have to learn from someone who doesn't even speak English?" But just like consultants are more valued if from out of town, a sensei trained from the direct line of Toyota masters is probably more knowledgeable and at the least engagingly inscrutable.

In some instances, a sensei can set up a good cop-bad cop scenario. A sensei will not appeal to some employees; if so challenge them to prove they can do as well. Use their uncertainty or negativity to everyone's advantage.

Enhance the sensei's impact by having staff question and answer periods, presentations about the progress of the organizations and special mentor relationships with selected staff. Integrate the sensei as a special, honored team member (suggestion: use the four-part teaming model to make this happen).

Near the end of the sensei dependency period, make it clear that the organization has grown so well, it is time to leave the nest. Celebrate the progress, mourn the change, and identify what each team member can contribute in the sensei's absence.

The mantle of Lean Thinking guru is transferred from Sensei to the Lean promotion department and then to managers and line staff who are becoming the primary change agents.

O

The Kaizen Department

A continuous improvement department or perhaps a kaizen promotion office is an important and necessary step to implement Lean Thinking. The questions to ask are: How big should it be and for how long should it operate?

One approach is that this department can grow to around five percent of the company workforce and be a permanent fixture.

Initially, a separate improvement department is necessary to initiate such a large change as Lean Thinking. However, this department can neglect respect for people opportunities and quickly decay into process improvement only.

Members of this new and elite Lean department can become narrowly trained experts who flood the organization's other departments with their expertise, tools, clipboards, stopwatches and other waste detectors. The focus is on improving the numbers. These people quickly become directors rather than teachers and coaches. This tendency can be easily overcome if the continuous improvement department continues to improve itself.

Once Lean momentum has been established, members of this office should become Lean consultants trained to join other departments for a substantial length of time, months if not a year or more. These consultants sit or stand with other workers, listen more than measure, discuss how to understand value and waste from all perspectives, begin improvement experiments, create or teach tools as needed, endorse fail-forward-fast efforts and become a team coach/sensei.

Where possible, the improvement office should join with the organization development office, where the real people skills often lie.

Common sense declares that every positive has a negative, every asset can be a liability, every move forward increases exposure to threat. Continuous improvement can step on the very people doing the work. Don't let it step on yours.

The continuous improvement department should grow like the people, not so much in size but in quality. Define continuous improvement and respect for people goals and measure progress.

o

Reporting Results

Both process improvement and people growth should be reported to the organization.

The data should include problems addressed, goals, tools used, which tools were most useful, the pre and post measures, what participants learned, what the home team learned, who turned from skeptic to fan, the biggest mistake and how customers (both paying and paid) received more value.

How should these data be reported?

If your organization is small enough, a presentation of your Lean efforts should be made to all staff regularly. If your organization is too large for this, divide presentations into two separate ones, leaders/managers and selected staff, or three parts, managers, selected staff and senior leadership. A workgroup presentation to senior leaders would add cachet.

The reports must be interesting and relevant; no long lists of data, minimal slides if any, good presenters rather than poor ones, enough time to tell the story and not so much to tell everything that was attempted and accomplished. Presentations should flow, perhaps with a theme to tie them together, and attendance should not be mandatory. If the quality is there, people will come. If people don't come, they haven't learned the value of Lean yet and/or your presentations are not good. Attendance is not the problem. Fix what is. Promote the reports. People will want to come to learn what they value.

As the organization matures and specific improvement events are no longer the primary effort, presentation should be in workgroups or departments. Senior leaders can attend.

When workgroups are implementing Lean, ideas, efforts, successes and failures should be formally and informally shared with similar workgroups across the organization.

Reporting results is a way of letting employees know how well their efforts are working; it also teaches and encourages. Make them relevant to adult learners, maybe even entertaining.

○

Process vs. People Improvement

In most companies, Lean Thinking quickly becomes focused on process improvement. Process improvement is easier, more obvious, measurable and seemingly more profitable and transferable than people improvement.

People get taken for granted.

This occurs because commonly available Lean experts don't know how to effectively include respect for people as they apply Lean tools.

The solution is amazingly simple. *Measure respect for people as much as you measure continuous improvement.*

Measure the big things: Is every employee trained sufficiently to do the job successfully?

Measure the middle things: How often do workgroups suggest an improvement idea?

Measure the small things: Can every employee access the boss when needed?

Monitor what is important:
- Do employees end most days satisfied?
- Are employees learning new skills?
- Are employees giving adequate feedback?
- Is every employee part of a team?
- Is the turnover rate low?
- What's the percentage of internal promotion?

And anything and everything else that emerges that leaders and employees think is important.

As a leader, if you prepare the people, respect the people and grow the people, you'll be doing your people side of Lean Thinking job. Measure and publicize how well this is going.

○

Dealing with *Concrete Heads*

Not everyone can become a change agent, not all change agents will follow the same route—not all have to march to the same drummer.

Implementing Lean Thinking can have a revolutionary effect, but not always one that is good. At some point in just about any revolution, the dynamic comes into play of, "You're either for us or against us." This is when you can lose a lot of good people.

One of the reasons you spent so much time and effort building high-performing teams is to better face the reality that some people get it, some people don't get it, and some are actively against it.

Your job is to worry only about the ones who are actively against the Lean effort. A few of the resisters you can help see Lean implementation differently, some you can neutralize and any remaining you will have to help find other pursuits.

Individually or in small groups, discuss the goal of maximizing value for the customers and see what happens. If they are for the goal, but uncertain that Lean is the best approach, agree that the proof will be how well Lean works. Give them time, information and results.

If they still do not see the value, discuss how they can still be an asset to the company. If this is possible, find them the right spot. If not possible, make sure they go quickly as they cannot function as a member of the team.

Concrete head is a term I learned from the Japanese senseis. I like the image for someone who doesn't want to get it. But remember it takes a while for concrete to set. Don't give up too soon.

People are critical of Lean Thinking when they don't understand it or have another approach that they prefer. Once they learn what Lean can do, they're fine.

For those who have a more entrenched rejection, often this is a control issue and not something to combat. Don't judge too soon. People take a while to adapt. If they are not doing harm, they probably will become assets soon enough. Allow them time to grow.

○

Employment for Life

Toyota became less attractive to investors when it essentially promised employment for life. It took this step as a natural and necessary demonstration of respect for people. Would a struggling employee be truthful if the probable outcome was losing the job? And would a good employee keep improving processes until the job was made redundant? "No" to both. Lean Thinking tools are designed to expose waste. We need employees to use these tools as well as possible and to freely point out waste as they see it or produce it.

In manufacturing, it is not overly difficult to find jobs for just about anyone. Where experience, safety or customer service is critical, sliding the wrong person or an incompetent one into the job could be ruinous.

Use the power of the team, especially the sense of membership and influence on the team. Faltering employees can be counseled in how certain behavior is negative for the team and how it impedes their work on behalf of the customer. The team is encouraged to help. Often the employee will work to improve, request a change to a more appropriate job or recognize that this company is probably not a good fit.

o

Manager/Teacher

We've focused on the respect for people pillar of the Toyota Production System. However, this pillar is only one of two, both of which support a wide and complex system of improving processes and people all the time.

It doesn't take much thought to realize that improving something requires deciding that the current way of doing things isn't good enough. For continuous improvement, what isn't good enough is the value-added percentage of the processes. How should we conceptualize what isn't good enough for the respect for people pillar?

I think it's the value-added percentage of fulfilling each employee's potential. We need to know how well people are becoming the best workers and change agents they can be.

The person to support fulfilling potential is the manager.

Most managers simply oversee employees, not guide them to experiment with how they do their jobs. Few of today's employees would seek out the boss to tell them of some failed experiment to improve the work. Yet we want both the experiment and the truth telling. It's up to the manager to make that happen.

Managers must be first and foremost teachers of Lean Thinking. This means creating teams that function well together, that can define standard work and that are continuously trying new ways and sharing results.

The bottom line to achieve this is a set of managers who guarantee every employee the safe environment necessary to challenge current thinking and current ways of getting the work done, including management.

Every employee should be well trained in:
- Supporting the team
- Identifying waste
- Finding the root cause
- Applying Lean tools
- Keeping a kaizen mindset

and be continually encouraged to do these on-the-job tasks by the manager.

Managers should see the work with their own eyes, be readily available and teach thinking skills. Coaching should be done frequently. Feedback should be constant, from everyone to everyone.

○

Time

Remember the medical assistant who took extra time from standard work to help a needy patient? Time is the critical measure for Lean Thinking. It is equally important for the people side of Lean but in a different way.

For your employees, value trumps time. This is true when employees meet customers' needs and when management meets employees' needs.

That assistant realized that making the effort to help the patient was adding value in spite of taking more time. She understood that time is a measure of efficiency, which is only a portion of adding value. Adding value directly, as the assistant did, is timeless.

Time and standard work were not the important measures, value was.

It would be absurd to ask: What is the management takt time for my employees? Yet that is exactly what happens when a 30-minute employee review is scheduled. You only have so much time and so many employees. You do the math and fit them into your schedule, just like cogs in a wheel, which they are not.

You should be efficient in your use of time, but not use time as the measure of when to start and stop contributing management value to your employees.

Of course, honor people by starting meetings on time and ending them on time as well. However, if someone needs more of your time give it to them.

Take whatever time is necessary to create value for employees; then get increasingly more efficient at doing it.

○

More to Do Checklist

Leaders are working together to improve
publicly declared management skills. ☐

Company Lean gurus have learned how to
coach. ☐

All employees are acquiring value-increasing
skills. ☐

Late adapters are supported. ☐

Inadequate team members are helped to find
more appropriate opportunities. ☐

Process and people improvement are equally
valued and reported on equally as well. ☐

Kaizen grows from formal and broad-scoped to
self-directed and local. ☐

Employees enjoy significant work security. ☐

Managers view teaching as one of the most
important components of their work. ☐

Managers use best practice management tools. ☐

Employees are increasingly fulfilling their
potential. ☐

Conclusion

I have used the word "should" about 114 times so far, not including the one in this sentence. When I was in graduate school, we students discussed the concept of the "tyranny of the shoulds," in the context of people being constrained by outside expectations.

What should you be doing? Who should you listen to? Ohno tells us to see with our own eyes, but for the people side of Lean Thinking, that isn't enough. We must see with everyone's eyes.

This book proposes that you can truly utilize the tools and power of Lean Thinking *only* if you partner with your people and execute that partnering as well as you pursue continuous improvement.

A BIT MORE

Appendix

What If

My wife and I were enjoying lunch on a sunny day sitting on a restaurant deck overlooking Puget Sound. We were at the water's edge watching the comings and goings of ferries and pleasure boats and dozens of people fishing off a nearby dock.

The two couples at the next table were tourists. They asked their waiter what the people were fishing for.

"I'm not sure," he said. "Maybe crab."

"Dungeness?" they asked.

"I'm not sure, but probably."

"How long is the season?" they wanted to know.

"I'm not sure about that either," he said. "Your guess is as good as mine." He took their order and left.

My wife and I agreed that the conversation was certainly amiable, but the chances were slim that he would take the time to learn the answers to their questions. This was a missed opportunity to provide better customer service and a missed opportunity for continuous improvement.

But what if…

What if the server knew about *value streams*?

If the server recognized that the questions from his customers were steps along the value stream, he would not have ignored the consequences of not knowing the answers to their questions. He would have realized that this was a non-value-added interaction, one that could easily be changed into a value added activity.

Elsewhere (*Earn Their Loyalty*) I talk about the value of internal virtual customers. I think that a virtual value stream residing in the heads of employees is an effective tool for fostering continuous improvement.

What if the sever had been taught about *innovation*?

He might focus on the interaction with his customers, noticing that he could not respond to their needs. He might ask himself how a fisherman would have handled the questions. Maybe he would wonder about the many types of questions customers were likely to ask.

He could share his concerns with other servers, maybe brainstorm a bit. They would certainly come up with better ways of responding to customer questions.

What if the server recognized the difference between a *job and making a contribution*?

He would pause for a moment after placing their order and wonder if he could have done more. He might dash to a nearby computer and look up what the current fishing season included. Or, he might ask others if they knew what the people on the dock were fishing for.

No matter how he found the answers, he would do what it took to find those answers and return with both the food and a bit of information.

What if the server was part of a team created using the *Four-Part Teaming Model*?

As a team member at this restaurant, the server would know that he was valued in part for his high-quality customer service. Thus, he would be especially sensitive to any indication that he had not met his customers' every need. Not having the answers to their questions would stand in stark contrast to his usual service.

He would make sure to right this wrong immediately.

What if this server had been taught the importance of the *big picture*?

That day, or maybe later in the week, he might realize he had missed an opportunity and that the same thing might be happening at the restaurant chain's other locations, especially those on the water.

Almost without doubt, if he worked in a *Heroic Environment*, he would go to his boss and explain his lack of knowledge. Management would come up with a way of alerting the other locations.

What if the server knew the concept of *Harnessing the Speed of Thought*?

Perhaps while digging into his restaurant-supplied dinner of fish and chips, he would identify the issue as: Servers are probably missing opportunities to fully inform customers. He might decide the goal was: No customer question will go unanswered and all will be answered factually.

He would realize that one hurdle was the vast range of questions that might be asked and the difficulty of all servers knowing all the answers. He also would realize that maybe it was not such a big problem and maybe didn't warrant the mobilization of a lot of resources.

He could chat with other servers to come up with a few possible solutions and end up talking with his boss. His boss might suggest that each site respond in ways that worked for them. Maybe even make it a contest to find which location could list the most questions.

What if the server was inspired by the company *vision*?

If the company vision was, "Every customer will leave our restaurant satisfied in every way," he might focus on how his inability to answer the couples' questions left them unsatisfied.

He would do whatever it took to rectify the situation.

What if the server knew how to determine *value*?

He would examine the unanswered questions from the customers' point of view. How important for an enjoyable lunch was it to know who was fishing for what? If he was quick enough, he could ask the customers themselves.

He probably knew without asking that ready answers would add value. With that in mind, he'd do what it took to ensure that he and others were adding value.

What if the server knew *kaizen*?

Maybe while drinking an iced tea during break, he would review his afternoon to see what could be improved. He would quickly focus on when he felt uncomfortable—being asked questions for which he had no answers.

He would immediately understand the problem and know the solution. By sharing his experience with others, they might have additional questions to answer and, together, create a quick way to teach one another and create more value for their customers.

What if the server knew the effect of *stories*?

Not only would the server know the answers to his customers' questions, he'd sprinkle his response with a few facts: the largest crab caught, where the restaurant found its crabs, the great storm that tore apart the restaurant a few years earlier and the whales that one could often see from the deck.

He would know how much to say so customers could enjoy the experience without their food getting cold or overstaying his welcome.

What if your employees thought this way and did these things?

○

The Chalk Circle

To help managers learn to see waste, Taiichi Ohno would draw a small chalk circle on the shop floor and have them stand in the circle, sometimes for a lengthy period, watching the production process.

You should do something similar on the people side. Figuratively draw a circle around your chair, in a hallway, at the table in a meeting.

Watch leaders in action. Are they inspiring or boring? Do they intimidate or support? Are they creating high-performing teams or leading a ragtag bunch of workers?

Observe a meeting. Are participants working together to assemble answers or discussing and re-discussing the issues? Are ideas captured on a white board or left in the air to swirl into oblivion? Is the best answer discovered or do votes determine the course of action?

Listen as a committee meets for the first time. Is a team created? How do they determine if the right people are attending? Do they decide the best ways to work together?

There are many areas full of NL activities on the people side. Leadership is one. Group problem-solving another. Team building a third. So is communication and even the degree of emotional engagement.

Sit or stand in the chalk circle. Lean to see the near invisible people side NL activities. With greater awareness, you will be able to enhance the second pillar of the TPS.

○

A Few Extras

In a well written article in *The New Yorker* magazine (Personal Best, Oct. 3, 2011), surgeon Atul Gawande wondered how he could improve as a surgeon and how others, such as athletes, musicians and teachers, could likewise improve.

You may remember this box from the first section on Focus.

Becoming a Lean Leader:

Leader ----------▶ Teacher

Teacher ----------▶ Student

Student = Learning = Change

You must change to become an effective Lean Leader

Perhaps like Dr. Gawande, you have been wondering how you can significantly enhance your skills as a Lean Leader. He found that having a coach improves most people's performance.

If you believe that you must become a teacher by first becoming a student and that you must learn how to manage differently and better than you have before; and if you realize that this means changing, you could use a coach.

Let's say you and your leadership team decide to embrace the information in this book and want to eliminate the waste in your behavior. Let's also say you decide you want to achieve five goals:

- A high level of measured productivity
- "Mistake-proofed" leadership
- High functioning teams
- High levels of staff satisfaction
- Daily process improvements

You then list some of the tools you'd like to learn to use:

- Lean principles (e.g., flow) applied to leadership
- Four-Part Teaming Model and Patrick Lencioni "dysfunctions" (From *Five Dysfunctions of a Team*)
- Effective presentations (informational, persuasive, etc.)
- Developing direct reports; FYI book (See Resources)
- Crucial Conversations
- Harnessing the Speed of Thought
- Time management, Covey Model

As a group, you decide a few tools in practice would look something like this:

- Use Four-Part Teaming model and Lencioni to create teams
- Use appropriate specific agendas to run meetings
- Use appreciative inquiry to discuss change in groups
- Operate work units from engaging vision statement and personal mission statements

- Operate teams from team agreements and peers holding each other accountable

How are you going to do all this? Find a coach.

As Dr. Gawande explains in his article, a coach can significantly improve a seasoned surgeon or teacher by being an informed set of eyes and ears, noticing actions and interactions and providing feedback with videotape accuracy. Such information can be invaluable, and humbling.

If we expect employees to embrace visual controls of their work, wouldn't it be inspiring for them to sit in a meeting with you, with your coach taking notes in a corner, and then join the coach in reviewing how you led the meeting? Everyone would learn a lot and the next meeting would be a much improved one.

Operating from the rule-of-thumb that 50 percent of any process is waste frees us from having to defend our actions. Of course, what we do can be improved. Accept that and the next step is easy: *Do whatever we can to improve.* My suggestion is to be as transparent as possible and to enlist the aid of everyone to help find the best ways to develop your skills.

It is beyond the scope of this book to present a comprehensive management approach, but this is something leaders must consider when implementing Lean or any significant change. In addition to maximum transparency, more efficient management will include policies that mandate Lean behaviors such as never passing defects and expecting employees to stop the line whenever necessary. There also should be a daily management system defined and in place to ensure that managers are alongside employees while they do the work and support them in their Lean efforts. Lastly Lean management must forgo traditional departmental silos replacing them with attention and accountability for the complete value stream.

The people side of Lean Thinking does not have to be a search for the one and only best way of creating value. As with process improvement, you can try many concepts and tools to reduce waste and instability and improve flow and value for the people side of Lean Thinking. Choose a tool, try it out, get feedback from employees and keep improving. It isn't rocket science, it's working together.

○

Recommended Resources

Lean Thinking

Lean Thinking 4.0, 2019 Robert Brown
Learn how to apply Lean to people interactions.

Lean Thinking, 2003, James P. Womack and Daniel T. Jones
The basic book on Lean Thinking and probably the best place to start.

Toyota Production System, 1988, Taiichi Ohno
A view of the early days. Necessary to truly understand the underpinnings of Lean Thinking; filled with jewels of wisdom.

The Toyota Way, 2004, Jeffery Liker
This book is an easier read than others and yet is a comprehensive presentation of the ideas.

The Lean Primer (www.Leanprimer.com), Craig Larman and Bas Vodde
The best description of both pillars and TPS I have seen.

Change

The HST Model for Change, Robert Brown
How to ensure everyone is productive involved in organizational change from start to finish.

The Heart of Change, 2002, John Kotter
Start here to understand organizational change.

Transitions, 2004, William Bridges
A tour de force about the emotional dynamics of change.

Management and Leadership

Mistake-Proofing Leadership, 2008, Rudy F. Williams and Robert Brown
Shows how to apply Lean principles to improve leadership.

Transparent Management, 2008, Robert Brown
Teaches some of the most important tools to enable managers to be transparent, including a comprehensive look at the Four-Part Teaming Model and Harnessing the Speed of Thought.

Earn Their Loyalty, 2011, Robert Brown
How to emotionally engage employees and paying customers. Includes the 4Cs.

Just Culture, 2007, Sidney Dekker
A solid explanation of the kind of place at which everyone should work.

Better Thinking, Better Results, 2003, Bob Emiliani
Case studies about lean transformation from an expert and pioneer on Lean leadership.

Others worth a look

The Speed of Trust, 2006, Stephen M. R. Covey
Explains the importance of trust and how to make it happen.

Crucial Conversations, 2011, Kerry Patterson et al
How to resolve significant differences in an organized and visible way.

Influencer, 2007, Kerry Patterson et al.
Learn the elements of change and how to influence others to make it happen.

For Your Improvement,(FYI) 2009, Michael M. Lombardo and Robert W. Eichinger
A deeply detailed listing and explanation of leadership skills designed to help with development and coaching.

The Baptist Health Care Journey to Excellence, 2004, Al Stubblefield
A well written description of putting employees before customers and how well that can work.

Get Rid of the Performance Review, 2010, Samuel A. Culbert
He makes a good argument for making this happen.

Glossary

5S	A tool to improve the efficiency of the work place. It includes five words beginning with S (translations vary) Simplifying, Sorting, Sweeping, Standardizing and Self-Discipline.
Andon	A visual control device (often a light) to display the current situation.
Cycle Time	The amount of time to complete one defined unit of work.
Flow (diagram)	The (description of the) movement of a product through production without stoppages.
Kanban	A communication tool, often a small card indicating a need for re-supply.
Kaizen	To break apart and put together more harmoniously: continuous incremental improvement.
Lead time	The amount of time from order to delivery.
Level Loading	Ensuring there is just the right amount of work, not too much or too little.

Poka-Yoke	Designing the process so it is impossible to do incorrectly. Hose connections, for example, that can only work if they are the right hoses.
Pull	Opposite of pushing the work downstream. The downstream worker pulls the work when ready.
Rapid Process Improvement Workshop	Most often a three to five-day improvement effort for a specific process by six to twelve employees.
Socratic Question	Loosely defined, the kind of question that will stimulate a discussion toward finding the truth.
Spaghetti chart	The map of a product as it goes through production.
Takt Time	A German term. Describes the rhythm of customer demand. It is the available time for production divided by the rate of customer demand.
Value Stream	The sequence of activities to meet a demand including ordering, producing and delivering.
Visibility Wall	A place, usually a wall, that holds descriptions of the most current kaizen data.

Index

Acknowledgments

I was certified as a Lean leader by John Black and Associates. His approach seemed like hell week at times, but I learned a lot from his efforts. I also had the pleasure of being mentored by the senseis of Shingijutsu, most notably Chihiro Nakao. This experience tied me directly to the historic Japanese method of learning — trial by expectation: Why improve a process by 10% when you can improve it by 90%, so go out and do it.

I was also fortunate to be part of the first nine years of Lean implementation at the Virginia Mason Medical Center in Seattle. My experience there was the stimulus for this book. During much of this time I was a member of the Clinic Kaizen team whose members, John Eusek, Liz Dunphy, Ann Kernan, Alenka Rudolph, Amy London, Amy Tufano, Gail Sausser, Jolyn Suko, Leanne Lewis, Trudie Read, Arni Verkler, Christine Day, and Cindy Rockfeld, taught me a great deal.

There were others from the Kaizen Promotion Office too: Miwa Kudo, Steve Gross, Susie Creger, Becky Foley, Chris Backous, Joan Naputi, Karen Gifford, Katerie Chapman, Linda Hebish, Robbi Bishop, Rosemary King, Rosemary Temple and Valerie Ferris and others who added to my knowledge.

In addition, I want to thank Diane Miller who hired me into the Organization Development department and my colleagues Rudy Williams, Marlenna Peppler, Steve Stahl and Thomas Nielsen. I learned so much from this team I will never be able to thank them enough. I was stretched, humbled, supported and warmly cared about.

I valued every minute and am still sad that our team had to disappear.

Another note on my colleague Rudy Williams. He was instrumental in developing my thinking about Lean and leadership. We have met frequently over the past two years to discuss how we can contribute to advancing Lean leadership development.

And another gang of people deserves mention for their support and inspiration. They are: Walt, Debbie, Wanda, Doug, Joanne, Amanda, Randy, Sharon, John, Christy, George, Danielle, Bev, Joan, Robyn, Richard, Jocelyn, David, Susan, Jane, Marcia, James, Tim, Lisa, Bror, Ginny and Kevin.

Dozens of others, too many to mention by name, were instrumental to my development as a reasonably good coach and mentor.

My editor, Gretchen Houser also deserves thanks. Any errors that remain are my doing; I can't resist a few late changes just before printing.

I thank you too, reader. My thoughts about what you need and the complex problems and delicate solutions you face, inspired me to gather information and put it together in what I hope is the most useful format.

About the Author

Bob Brown lives with his wife and numerous animals north of Seattle. In addition to a few salaried jobs, Bob has been an independent performance enhancement coach for over thirty-five years. His expertise lies in helping individuals and groups achieve their highest good. He spends his time consulting, leading Lean and leadership development workshops, coaching and writing.

His undergraduate degree is from the University of Michigan, his doctorate from the United States International University, and he has pre and post-doctoral training from the University of Michigan Neuropsychiatric Institute.

He is president of Collective Wisdom, Inc.

Bob's recent books. Available on Amazon.com and other outlets.

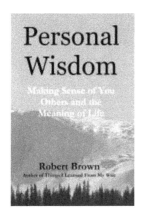

The book covers a lot of territory, including how to become perfect.

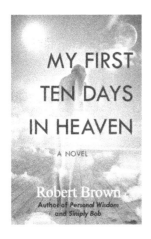

An atheist finds himself in Heaven and wonders who made the mistake.

How to make emotional and logical sense of change so everyone wants to be on board

Treating employees and customers so everyone wins.

COLLECTIVE
WISDOM INC

None of us is as smart as all of us.

Please visit www.collwisdom.com

or

www.Robert-Brown-Books.com

CPSIA information can be obtained
at www.ICGtesting.com
Printed in the USA
FSHW022004120619
59019FS